BEYOND THE WALLS 2025

Beyond the Walls 2025

NEW WRITING from YORK ST JOHN UNIVERSITY

VP

VALLEY PRESS

First published in 2025 by Valley Press
Woodend, The Crescent, Scarborough, UK, YO11 2PW
valleypressuk.com

ISBN 978-1-915606-61-7
Cat. no. VP0248

Cover illustration by Aimee Wade.
Cover and text design by Jamie McGarry.

Printed and bound in Great Britain by
Imprint Digital, Upton Pyne, Exeter.

Contents

Foreword

'The mind is its own place, and in itself
Can make a Heaven of Hell, a Hell of Heaven.'
– John Milton, Paradise Lost (Book 1: ll. 254-5)

The mind is not a quiet place. It's a restless, kinetic organism. It thrashes, folds, unravels, and refashions itself. It is both an engine of meaning and a house of mirrors distorting our world and our sense of our place in it. In reading *Beyond the Walls* 2025, it becomes clear that the mind is not just a container for thought, more a terrain we traverse.

This year's anthology takes as its theme The Mind, and, like the best explorations, it does not chart easy paths or offer simple consolations. Instead, the writers gathered here confront the mind's complexity. Their work leads us through hallucinations and insomnia, through grief, recovery, and those strange, quiet hours when life itself feels like a memory we are only half-living. There are moments of humour here, flashes of savage clarity, and the dense, pulsing emotions that language struggles, and sometimes fails, to contain.

One striking thread you will find woven here is the sense of dislocation – from others, from self, from certainty. There is an almost unbearable intimacy in the small kinds of failures that the poetry and fiction herein explores. These writers take us into the body's betrayal of the mind, and vice versa.

But this anthology does not dwell solely in darkness. It also bears witness to the mind's resilience – for finding or creating paths back to meaning. Like I've done in my own writing, some pieces here explore how physical movement can become a form of cognitive rescue, balm even. Running becomes an act of mindfulness (it was so for humans long before mathematics, stories, perhaps even language). Movement, and running in particular is a way of performing one's being in the world, of attuning oneself to its textures and the flicker of experience. Running here is not heroic; it is humble, intimate, and profoundly moving. It reminds us that the mind's health is stitched into our body's experiences, that endurance can be learned, and that some battles are fought one careful step at a time.

Several pieces deal directly with violence – but not always the kind we might expect. Rage, guilt, trauma, all churn beneath the surface, of the poetry and prose here – sometimes manifesting as hallucination, sometimes as memory, sometimes as physical dread. Some of these stories are unsparing and offer no easy exoneration, no simple moral tidy-up at the end. But it is precisely their refusal to simplify that endows them with powered resonance. They show the mind as it often is: raw, conflicted, endlessly inventing and revising reality.

The writing collected here is shot through with the understanding that to have a mind is to be vulnerable. Every piece acknowledges, implicitly or explicitly, that the mind's most potent acts are not those of calculation or conquest, but of connection to other minds and to the world.

In *Beyond the Walls* 2025, the mind is revealed in all its glorious contradictions. It is a festival of selves. These writers show us that the mind, like Milton's Heaven and Hell, is not merely a place we inhabit, but something we shape, for better or worse, with every thought, every memory, real or imagined. To have a mind is to live at the mercy of its power, to endure it, yes, but also to revel in its creativity. It is a privilege to accompany these writers as they venture beyond the safe walls of certainty, beyond the walls of our academy, and the city, to confront the mind's mysteries head-on. I invite you, reader, to do the same: to step beyond your own walls, to risk being unsettled, and to discover what new worlds your mind might yet create.

Prof. Vybarr Cregan-Reid,
York St John University

Preface

The journey to putting this anthology together has not only been insightful and illuminating but has also showed everyone involved what it feels like to really pursue their passions. It has truly been rewarding to say the least. Working with people from different backgrounds, but who are all like-minded in their love for creative writing and publishing, ended up being a fusion of intense creativity and determination which has resulted in the anthology being what it is today.

Coming up with this year's theme of 'The Mind' was our first challenge as an editorial team, but once we decided on it, we knew that the standard of submissions this year was going to be more than just impressive. We believe that 'The Mind' is interpretative and inclusive and represents an array of great emotion, perspectives, and experiences that we are incredibly proud to share. We wanted to capture unique voices which told powerful stories taken from their deepest thoughts, their hidden identities, perplexing dreams, fears, and anxieties. Our anthology, as a result, hosts a vibrant array of memories and emotions that reflect the complex vision of the mind itself.

Each submission has been carefully curated by the authors and polished to the best standard by this year's phenomenal editorial team who have taken extra care to refine every minor detail before publication. As editors, we have ensured that a strong sense of devotion has been shown to each piece within the anthology. We have worked tirelessly to improve our skills and create a true sense of the mind through the intricate, written word.

Everyone involved in this year's project has put so much effort and drive into promoting this anthology, with unique events showcasing the exceptional talent here at York St John University. Our social media has reached new heights, with visibility and interactions showing what this project means to the writing community established on campus and beyond, and this is all thanks to the brilliant work of our marketing and events team. Continually, the blogs and podcasting team have created inspiring content in the run up to the publication of the anthology, discussing publishing, what this year's anthology is all about and more.

Each individual on this year's *Beyond the Walls* team has put their everything into this anthology and we are so excited to share it with the world. We want to give our deepest thanks and appreciation to the writers who submitted their writing, the Creative Writing school at York St John who have been so supportive throughout the process of this year's anthology and everyone at Valley Press for collaborating with our team. You have all helped us make something remarkable. We hope you enjoy exploring each page, all which link together to form our version of 'The Mind'.

Becca Green,
Editorial Team Leader

Consumption of Detachment

it begins with the wilting and withering of the wildflowers

weeds unravelling
twisting through your fingers
the sting of the nettle goes unfelt
and the stab of the thistle isn't worth a gasp

tests designed to see if you are hollow inside

and soon the vines will crawl over your body
daring to pry your skull apart
a pomegranate splitting
spitting crimson

your body will rot in this earth

where the wildflowers will revive and
you will finally be at peace
once you lay in the bellies of the beasts

for you wandered too far this time
and now you've lost your way.

Sophie Marlowe

Awakening

You wake up to blinding lights, as if your eyes never closed in the first place, it hurts. Your bed doesn't feel comfortable anymore, why did you spring for memory foam, you whine. In fact, your quilt has become heavy, numbing. You try to get up – reposition yourself some way comfortable. You can't. Despite what your brain is signalling, your eyes won't shut either. The light is awful, all encompassing; the room, the blankets, the mattress, the pillows have all evolved beyond numbness: into searing pain – you feel it all over, from the tips of your toes to the top of your head. Why can't I move, you agonise, what's happening to you? You try to scream, but your mouth won't open – or is it already open? You can't tell. All you know is you can't make a sound. You can't let loose the agonies you feel that remain rattling inside you. Nobody can hear the anguish you endure; nobody will come and save you from this horrible awakening. This anguish is something very few have experienced and fewer still have lived. You are afraid. Afraid of what you know will come.

An end.

Why does this scare you?

When a nervous system is exposed to anything outside the body in which it inhabits: it, for lack of better words, experiences sensations that are unlike anything anyone can ever feel; it is unbearable. If you were to somehow survive the ordeal of having your nervous system extracted and placed into the world, you would be longing for your life to end within the hour. Now you understand why you would want to make that choice of your own volition – or wishing you could in any case.

Miraculously your eyes, your globular little sensory nodes, have adjusted to the blinding light, yet they cannot move. They are locked, staring into the mirror directly in front of your bed, and there you lay, or at least what you believe to be you. Unblinking, you stare, your eyes begging for any kind of liquid, into that mirror. And as they dry out, they etch and burn this final sight into themselves: an image of a tangle of nerves unspooled on the bed, tangled around themselves, under and over the bedding, topped off by a pair of loose eyeballs sunk into the 1.4 kilograms of putty-like muscle. You.

Slowly you wither away, granted nothing but your sense of sight and thoughts. You won't get the chance to say your final words, and you won't get the chance to draw your final breath either. You will simply continue to experience the agonies of oxygen and carbon and nitrogen atoms repeatedly smashing into your nerves, feeling every part-per-million crash into every part of you. You will feel gravity pulling you into your bed sheets, and your quilt being pulled onto you, increasing the area of which your nerves touch something, your brain screaming at you, at itself, to move – to escape from the pain. Your only mercy comes when the brain can no longer compute the signals being shot at it, your neurons stop firing, stop issuing commands to where your lack of muscles would be. At which point you are acutely aware that your time is coming to an end. Which can only be described as ecstasy, nirvana, reaching a higher plane of being – from feeling everything, more than one should ever feel, to feeling nothing. Experiencing nothing. You long for it to end and yet you're fearful of it. Why? All of your problems will be solved, there will be no pain, no worries, no conscious decisions to make. Why are you afraid of the solution?

You awake in the same room, you are still blinded as if you never shut your eyes, you still feel numb from the morning. Yet, you get up. You move. You live.

Ethan Clark

Your Perception

Translucent skin hangs off your bones like a
cracked, sandpapery, leather jacket that
wears too big for your petite frame.
Liver spots darken your skin, it ripples over your muscles
moving with my hand as I soothingly stroke your arm.
You weep into the crook of my neck about how
'this and that' is not fair!

Cured with a hot cuppa, newspaper, choccy biscuits
your hazy eyes meet mine and, with a sweet toothless smile,
you thank me wholeheartedly for my kindness.

I crouch beside you.
'You are beautiful,' you tell me.
'Your teeth are so straight, your eyes so pretty
your skin so clear.'
Envy seeps from you
your wrinkled finger strokes my bare cheek.

You caress my hair, commenting on how bonny I look.
You do not believe me when I say how beautiful you are,
yes your skin is falling off your skeleton
but your eyes are alive with accomplishments that
I can only dream of.

Jealousy for each other is paramount.
We are beautiful but
all you see is my youth.

Elle Hartley Smith

The Little Village of Woodencreek

The little village of Woodencreek had always been cursed. Or so the locals had whispered. Young girls and boys were often born as curse-holders, their bodies vessels for the dark spirits who lurked in the woodlands just at the edge of their town, waiting to get in. Waiting to find a host. The spirits would outlive the host, of course. Maybe they would go back to the shadowy forest where they had come from, or maybe they would haunt the family, waiting with a hungry smile, biding their time until the next child was born. That is what the village people had whispered the day that Enola Cartwright had been born, a crying wriggling mass in her cot, all swaddled in pink hand-knitted blankets. Enola Cartwright had been cursed by the spirits of The Great Beyond. The village folk had danced and thrown strange herbs around her crib on the night of her birth. They had tried everything to kill the spirit, sighing in relief when they believed it to be gone. Enola's father had shaken their hands, bowing and ushering them from the room with hushed praises and thank yous. However, Enola's father had known the truth. He had known that Enola Cartwright was and always would be cursed.

Enola had often sat outside on her porch as a little girl, rubbing her hands together anxiously beneath the chorus of the wind chimes above her. She would stretch her little legs in front of her, letting the river water rush over her bare toes as she became absorbed with her own thoughts. Her father would watch her for a while, his brows furrowed before joining her.

'What are you thinking, Enola? What's going on inside that big head of yours?' he would ask her. Enola would always smile, giggling, her wet feet pattering off the decking as she ran over to hug him. He had always asked that question for as long as she could remember. Perhaps he had been afraid at the idea of what kind of thoughts circled within a cursed child's mind. She would usually make a slight humming sound, hearing her father's ringing thoughts in her head. The words were so crisp and clear. *Why isn't this child of mine happy? Why is this child of mine so constantly concerned?* Enola would shake the words from her head, her mind going silent.

'What's going on inside that big head of yours?' her father would repeat, crouching down and looking into her eyes with apprehension. It was as though he was inspecting her thoughts. It was as though he was checking that it was *Enola* that he was talking to. Her face would scrunch up with worry, her father sticking his tongue out at her and making her burst out in a fit of laughter. She would push his shoulder lightly as if to swat that silly expression from him before he would wrap her in a loose hug, sighing with relief. His daughter was still his. The curse had not yet taken her.

Enola had always felt so deeply and thoroughly. She had been an endless well of thought and sensitivity. Growing up, she had told her father this. Of how sometimes, she could hear people's thoughts in her head as if they were her own. On the day where she had first admitted this, her father had grabbed her by the shoulders and had told her sternly to never speak of it. To never tell a soul of her ability. She was gifted, that was all. Different. Special. And no matter what, she was to tell nobody of this power. Usually, this rant was followed by a story, one of which, by the end of her life, Enola had heard a thousand times and would even repeat to herself.

'Your mother fell pregnant with you in the early spring. She had been happy and calm, but her heart had been heavy towards the end of her time growing you. She had become tired and weak and eventually it had become obvious that the sadness had infected you.' He would tell the story seriously and with great urgency. 'You wouldn't settle well in those first few weeks, so one day, I visited the markets. I went to the nearest fortune stall and paid the woman running it to tell me one of her fortunes. To tell me of your fate.' Enola's heart had always pounded at this part. 'She had told me that you were different. That your life was to be plagued by power. Strange power. Dark power.' He usually frowned here, taking a moment to consider his words. The village folk had advised that he drown her, forcing the spirit out of her. It would let her mind be her own once more, uninhabited by darkness. They had wanted to let her find peace. To put an end to her crying. To put an end to her suffering. 'I told them that you were strong and different and that they were speaking nonsense.' He would always cup Enola's face fiercely. 'I told them that I didn't believe them. I told them that you were *mine*.'

On her eighteenth birthday, Enola had fallen in love. He had been an outsider of the village, and not one to easily believe the stories of the cursed. He thought them to be fables. Wives' tales. *Nonsense.* As time had ticked by, their love had grown deeper. Deep enough that she had later married him. For Enola, however, she had first needed to tell him of her fate. Of the woman and the fortune stall. Of her mother and The Great Beyond. Of her secret. She had done it by the weeping willow creek, her hand intertwined in his, her feet dangling off the edge of a mossy outcropping, the river trickling past beneath them.

'You know I'm cursed, don't you?' she had asked. She had watched his face ticking through emotions, her hands fidgeting as they had done when she had been a child.

'Cursed?' he had asked. Enola had simply nodded, bowing her head in shame. Bowing her head to avoid seeing the expression that she had become so familiar with in her life. *Fear.* Instead, he had just shrugged, smiling dumbly. 'I don't mind.' His voice had been confident yet naïve, his face pink with flush as she had looked up at him. She had understood his next words before he had even spoken them. 'I love you,' he had confessed, skipping a flat rock over the water. 'I love you.'

'I love you too,' Enola had replied, feeling her heart racing, her soul coming alive. 'I love you very much,' she had repeated, though a singular thought had plagued her, running through her mind. Is it me who loves him, or the curse?

As time had gone by, this question had no longer mattered to Enola. The pair had married and become partners. Lovers. Friends. They had raised a family and grandchildren together. They had travelled and *lived* together, years of Enola's life flying by before she found herself an old woman, resting in her bed as she listened to the little windchimes twinkling outside of her childhood home once more.

* * *

Enola watched as the midday sun blazed down on the river just beyond her bedroom, her limbs aching with age. A small smile strained at her lips as her husband led her grandchildren into the room to see her, his hand resting shakily atop hers as she pulled herself upright.

'Let me tell you a story,' Enola began, her grandchildren listening with awe. 'Of the day that I was born.' Enola tried to ignore the pain within her as she spoke, but she couldn't. Earlier in the day, she had felt a hollowness that she had never experienced before. She had felt her spirit beginning to separate from her and she had known, that by midnight, it was going to abandon her. She had known that it was going to return to that place that only seemed to exist in the most worrying corners of her nightmares, and the thought had frightened her. She could still feel the creature now, beat for pulsing beat as its heart began severing from her own. She could feel the burning fibres of its soul as it began to pluck itself from her, her mind reaching out to stop it, begging it not to go, but it yearned to return to The Great Beyond once more. Its thoughts uttered for the final time in Enola's mind as she clutched her chest weakly at the pain. *Thank you for this good life,* it whispered. *Thank you for living with me.* Enola nodded silently, as she continued quietly with her story.

'My mother fell pregnant with me in the early spring,' she smiled bittersweetly, knowing that this was the final time that she would tell it. 'And the village people told me that I was cursed.'

Sophia Murphy

Ellipsis

Every sentence began and ended in ellipsis
The silence covers the room like eclipses,
Their words sound different, now you miss them.
Don't know how to start so you wish them... well.

Now you're just a B-side
To the people you used to know,
You're waking up happy as you rub your eyes,
They don't think of you, you can go be yourself now,

You move on to another city,
You contact some with a few fond memories
Better on your own, found your own beat,
Now you feel like an A-side,
A first time hit, played on repeat.

Ryan Williams

Wavelengths

Restless waves crash into the riptide,
how I love this kind of conversation.
Come closer and talk to me about your day,
whisper every little detail into my ear.

From the vibrations of your vocal
to the ripples of your voice.
Well I am happy to heed its call.
So I am never to stray
from this storm brewing all through my body.

We pull back so I can gaze
into those alluring coral eyes.
Filled with lust, they stun me.
Completely sedated unknown
if I may be drowning.
More so than I was when I stepped foot into this
once calming ocean.

May we both stand here forever,
and allow for these tempestuous waves
to crash into our bodies.
Become entangled with one another for all eternity?

But I know I should let these waves blow you away,
so you forever become evanescent with the winds.
But I will honour this treasure.
That I shall keep beside me for all time.

Rhiannon Thorley

My Love Letter to Summer

O Summer, sunshine, and sweltering heat,
How you revive me once I survive the bleak winter,
How you make walks outside a pleasant treat.

You force me to sit in my garden again,
Drowning out unruly neighbours and hedge trimmers
with earbuds, the uncomfortable wooden table – my perfect den.

You bless me with cherries, strawberries and tomatoes
   a-plenty,
From my dad's self-planted crops that crowd every corner,
Providing the bugs and snails with a free-for-all frenzy.

Each year, we always visit the same old places,
My grandma's house for one week, the Polish coast another,
Where we always get sunburned on our shoulders and faces.

We pack all the aloe vera, swimsuits, and mosquito repellent,
And crowd into our car for twenty-four long hours,
Trying to catch a wink on the ferry, that has never been silent.

Revisiting old memories has never been cheap,
But I always beg my parents to go together,
O Summer, I don't care if you melt my skin –
I will always be deeply in love with your weather.

Klaudia Ksiazkiewicz

Unravel

By 19, all I wanted to be was good. I'd been everything else. A misguided and vaguely pathetic sort of angst burning through my skin at all times, ears full of smoke drowning out anyone's words but mine. I already know, whatever you're about to tell me, I already know. I'd tell everyone to go away and shut up and stop talking to me oh my god. I was Effy Stonem, I was a lit cigarette. I was smudged eyeliner and vodka cordial and the weird stairs you have to go down when there's a fire alarm above the ground floor. I was intolerable. Embarrassed. So by nineteen, all I wanted to be was good.

No one liked Effy Stonem. Except for people who thought they were Effy Stonem. And no one likes those people, either. They grow out of that, eventually, and start thinking they're something else, start dressing corporate goth or become weirdly into protein smoothies. I didn't do any of that but that's because I'm different I'm better I'm the exception. I run a crochet club and I can't stop falling in love. And out of it. And in and out and in and out and that's it that's all I ever do. Usually with the same people.

To have loved and lost is better than not to have loved at all, or whatever it is they say to people who've just been dumped for the third time this year. There's this one guy, at the crochet club I run, who I've been in love with three times now. He's got messy hair and blue eyes and he always wears horrible funny t-shirts that say things like 'If you're reading this you're too close' on them. Last week he wore one that said 'I wonder if beer thinks about me too' and I wanted to go up to him and say something like wow I like your shirt haha but I got too in my head about it and instead didn't say anything at all. Just sort of looked at him for a bit while talking about how to do a stitch I actually don't know how to do myself. We've never properly spoken, you see. But I have been in love with him three times so far. I only stop loving him when he wears the shirt that has a picture of a tree on it and says, 'I need to shave my bush.'

I've also been in love with the girl who always sits next to him, I've decided they have sex sometimes in his car after crochet club. Which makes me incredibly jealous but wow I am so happy for them. I brought them together, you see. I don't know what it is about a slip stitch that renders them unable to wait until they get home to do that but yes I'm happy for them, I guess. She's beautiful though she really is, hair is the same brown as her eyes and her laugh sounds like birthday cake. I made her laugh, once. She was ten minutes late maybe a month ago, as she walked through the door I said hello missy what time do you call this, like I was her mum or something. She laughed and said ohhh if only I was as good at parallel parking as I am at crocheting, which I thought was odd because she can't drive, she made a joke once about how she can't drive, she doesn't have a licence. And also she isn't very good at crocheting. So I said oh I didn't know you could drive? And she just laughed again, like I was kidding but I wasn't. It didn't matter though, she could laugh in my face while running down all my fingers with a carrot peeler and it still wouldn't matter I think. With every laugh I picture being Damien, in his car with her. Need a lift home? I practice saying, over and over. Need a lift? Since you don't have a licence? No? Yes? Take off your shirt? What?

I'm not in love with her anymore, though. I've seen how she looks at Damien. While he's teaching her how to do a granny square because I was too busy looking at political memes on Twitter. She's not very good at crocheting but she knows how to do a granny square. She wants his hands on hers, his eyes too. I can't get in the way of that, I've brought them together I can't get in the way of that. It's desperate though, really. Laughs too hard at his t-shirts (even the bush one), laughs too hard at unfunny stories I'm sure she's already heard. Her laugh is different when it's for him. Flaccid.

They're the only people I've been in love with this year – from crochet club at least. Last year though I was in love hard. He loved me, too. We spoke every day, went to dinner sometimes, the classics.

He met my parents and I met his and then his parents met my parents and then we broke up. I got some new glasses, and he didn't like them or something. He also said we're fundamentally incompatible and I spend too much time thinking and doing absolutely fucking nothing and I need a hobby but I have a hobby and then he said not really and broke up with me and called me boring.

Which was cool.

We met at my crochet club, which he still goes to for some reason. He's still in love with me I think. I announced the breakup a month after it happened, just in case. Stood up in front of everyone, told them it was mutual and then started crying and had to excuse myself to 'go for a poo.' Damien and Jem looked extra smug when I walked back in, crossing their legs all funny as if to say wow you'll never get to do what we just did, in my car. In his car. In the car. I fell out of love with both of them then (I'd fallen back in love with Jem the week before because she wore purple eyeshadow and kept talking about how much she loves Battenburg), and I fell out of love with my ex, too.

I think I might disband crochet club. I hate it, actually. I've spent so much money on wool in the past two years and guess what I don't even know how to crochet. How funny is that, I don't even know how to crochet. I tell them the names of stitches I've found online and they kind of just figure it out from there. Damien how do you do it it's soooo hard. Yeah I bet it is. My ex knows how to crochet because he's so insanely insecure he thought he was just too stupid to understand the way I teach, so he'd always excuse himself and watch YouTube videos in the bathroom then come back and make a shit blanket or something. He wasn't too stupid to understand me, not in that sense anyway. In fact I am too stupid to understand myself, I think.

It's getting so stressful. I don't even know how to crochet. But I also don't know which t-shirt Damien is going to wear next week, so it's a real dilemma if that makes sense. I host it in my living room, so now whenever I'm in my living room I just feel like I'm at crochet club and I'm on edge like I should be teaching a room full of people something they already know. The blue carpet and blue wallpaper and blue sofa and blue and blue and blue. I might get into astrology, or class As? Something to pass the time. My only fear is that they carry on crochet club without me I think. In someone else's living room, and new people join and fall in love with each other and then out of love with each other and in and out and in and out. All while I'm at home reading my ex's birth chart high on crack I guess. I've been good. I buy wool from the old woman at the market instead of Hobbycraft, I think I've loved everyone at least once and I only drink decaf now too. I try and I try but I can never do it. I'm good and then I'm pretending I know how to crochet. These two people I don't even know are having sex in a car? In his car? The car? Everyone I know is at the mercy of my mind, if that makes sense. I blame the stars, the loved and the lost and the guy behind the counter at Lidl. Yes I need a bag with that. Do you want to go and have sex in a car? In my car? No?

Fair enough.

Eloise Stone

While it's in the Kiln

my face ripples
red in the water.

i cannot see my eyes.
i cannot see much at all.

passing colours and shapes
that somehow make up Me.

somehow more whole than
those pulled from the surfaces
of clear glass and silver lakes.

somehow i am a part of
the grit and grain and grime.
somehow it is part of Me.

i am not the clean and shining self,
washed-up and bright-eyed,
that stands before the hand mirror.

half-lit by the red flame of candlelight,
not the white sun of day, this is me:
murky and soil-soaked
unsure and stained.

i am staring down at a bucket of slip.
perhaps no one else would recognise
this watery reflection of mine,
but i do.

i am there,
in the soil and stain.
a reflection of my own;
water muddied
sculpted by my hand

this is Me.

Alice Lind-O'Mara

What a Drag

As a seven-year-old girl, who had already figured out that I was bisexual (thanks to Doctor Who and vampires), I was struggling with my femininity. I'd stopped wearing dresses to school, I was on the football team and the cricket team, and it was far easier to practice in trousers. Besides, I'd always been told I wasn't very graceful. I always forgot to cross my legs while wearing a skirt, always forgot I couldn't climb trees with the boys if I was in a dress. I loved being friends with the boys. One lunchtime, they said that Maddie was the coolest girl they knew, because she was 'basically a boy.' I was so jealous that I declared her my archnemesis. Not that she cared – she was better than me in almost every conceivable way: more popular, better at sports, and certainly far better at holding a conversation. I still hadn't quite developed the ability to successfully hold a conversation that didn't involve me rambling about one of my special interests. Maddie made me burn with jealousy.

As a twelve-year-old girl(?), I felt sick whenever anyone called me by name. I begged my mum to let me cut my hair. My hair was so long that it ran down to my thighs when down and sat low on my back when tied up. My mum told me I'd regret a haircut, but I knew what I wanted. My girlfriend (if you're willing to consider a secondary school relationship as real) had introduced me to the YouTubers Dan and Phil. When I like something, I cannot like it a normal amount. I was obsessed with them. I especially liked Dan. When my mum finally let me get a haircut, I knew how I wanted to look. I asked for my hair to be cut like Dan Howell, terrible emo fringe and all. Some of the only pictures of my pre-teen self with a smile were taken after that haircut. I felt like I was finally finding a real identity for myself, even if that identity was a patchwork made up of hair like Dan Howell, makeup like 2005 Gerard Way and fashion like 2013 Patrick Stump.

As a fourteen-year-old boy(?) who was still figuring out my identity and using secret social media accounts with fake names, I started wearing a binder for the first time. Getting paid only £4 an hour to be a waiter, I couldn't afford to order a real binder from a professional company. I ordered the cheapest binder I could find, £2 off of Amazon. My ribs will probably resent me for the rest of my life for that choice – to this day, even though I now wear body-safe binders, my ribs still ache.

As a sixteen-year-old boy, I was struggling with severe depression and trying to come to terms with the realisation that a lot of my body dysphoria was due to years of repeated sexual assault. I was desperate to find a way to express my femininity that didn't trigger all of the horrible feelings I had about my body. It was around this time that I was starting to obsess over RuPaul's Drag Race. Watching other queer people explore their own complicated gender expression through beautiful fashion made me envious. I wanted to be just like that. This was when I bought my first fashion design book. The first designs I created were not good. They were the messy scribbles of someone who did not know how fabric fell on a body. Slowly, however, I got better with practice, although I still cannot draw a shoe for the life of me. The first fashion design I was proud of was a pair of outfits themed after Greek gods, specifically Dionysus and Apollo. I was even prouder this year, at 22, to style my best friend in the Dionysus design, finally bringing it into the realm of reality. I only told him afterwards that the outfit he was wearing was such a fundamental early part of my gender discovery journey.

As a seventeen-year-old boy, I finally decided to try drag for myself. I picked a very cliché drag name which I will not share, for fear of someone dredging up ancient images of me as a baby queen. I looked utterly terrible, but I was proud of myself, and my mum was proud of me, and I adore her, so that was all that mattered to me.

When I came to university at eighteen years old, and had complete freedom to explore who I was without fear of judgement from the closed-minded people in my hometown, I started to realise that he/him pronouns weren't suiting me as comfortably as I'd thought. When people started to become confused about my gender, unsure how to refer to me, I began to realise what I liked. I liked ambiguity. I liked the absence of a solid gender identity, the fluidity of my expression, the freedom to present however I wanted to on any day without worrying about whether I was successfully passing as male or female. When I found the term non-binary, I loved it.

At nineteen years old, and performing in drag regularly, I was happy for a time until I realised that drag queens can be utterly horrible. As a broke university student, I couldn't afford expensive drag outfits, nor could I afford the materials to make them myself. Though I was working hard to make up for it with fun performances filled with stunts and reveals, having my drag called 'mediocre' at every show by people who were supposed to be my friends was starting to damage my mental health. At twenty years old, I quit drag, citing a need to protect my mental health. I was heartbroken that something so important to me had been ruined. I kept creating fashion designs, but I couldn't help but miss performing. During this time, I started to develop the network of friends that I have now, who I'm lucky are far more supportive than my old 'friends'. When I found my partner and we began to interact with each other's friends, I was lucky enough to be introduced to one of the most talented people I've ever met. I'd heard of them before meeting them. Oh, I had heard about Spikey Mikey's drag shows. I'm a very jealous person and expected to be horribly envious when I finally met them.

What I hadn't expected was how pleasant they'd be, how they'd encourage me to get back into drag on my own terms, to explore the world of drag kings and things, how they'd welcome me to their scene rather than excluding me like the queen scene had. I thought on what they told me for a while. I was terrified of starting drag again, scared that I'd crash and burn. It was scarier than the first time I started drag, because I could no longer carry my performances with stunts; chronic pain had taken away my ability to wow a room with a death drop or a split. At twenty-one years old, however, I was far braver than I was at seventeen. I came back with a new drag name to reflect my new identity, Percy Bitch Shelley. I explored my talents and found that I'd been trying far too hard to be a dancer when my real skill was singing, and oh boy, I love belting a show tune. I made a drag family for myself, and started running my own events – masquerade balls, Halloween parties, and a drag show of my own. An 'Event of the Year' award for one of my masquerades validated everything I wanted to feel about my drag; I am not mediocre. I am spectacular.

At twenty-two years old, I feel far more complete as a person. I feel validated, respected as a performer. I feel comfortable, I feel right in my identity as a non-binary person. I have gone through hell, and then I have gone through therapy, and come out on the other side able to accept that being assaulted through my childhood was not my fault and should not make me hate my body. I have people who love me, that I love in turn. Most importantly, I have a vision for my future, something I could never have imagined as a depressed sixteen-year-old. I did not think I'd be alive to see eighteen, but at twenty-two, my very existence is an act of revolution. Politicians wish to eradicate my way of life. They will not be given the privilege of destroying me.

Sebastian Forrester

Octopodia: An Encounter with the Octo-Self

An innate reaction takes over. Something has been sensed, a flash from the ocular to the Centre, danger. A command: implement strategy 1. A signal flares from the Centre, directing the Sub-centres, all 8 respond and move their attached muscles, gripping to a surface. Activate: pigment cells. The Centre is unaware of what this does, what happens when this instinct activates, but it is aware of the effect. The thing, whatever it is, whatever danger triggered this response, leaves the Centre alone, doesn't notice and moves on. This works, almost always, if it fails other strategies can be deployed, untested by the Centre, but instinctually effective.

The Centre sense-sees the danger gone: pigment cells deactivate. Signals out to the Sub-centres, they respond.

[Sub-centre 1 activate, forward grasp pull], [Sub-centre 2 activate, adjust for Sub-centre 1 grasp forward pull]

This happens simultaneously and results in the Centre moving, floating through the world across the floor. While the Sub-centres deal with this task the Centre can focus on hunting. The Centre begins speculative foraging, an un-picky shopper browsing the reduced aisle, everything a potential source of life. Ocular sweeps across the floor, waiting for something to trigger a response.

Ocular trigger: response sent to 4 Sub-centres, initiate. The Centre floats up, before plunging down, the 8 Sub-centres wrap around the thing. Each Sub-centre attaches, signals sent back to the Centre. A picture of the thing forms, a detailed analysis of it, strengths, weaknesses, and strategies to implement.

The Centre thinks, the Sub-centres wait. Initiate first extraction. Signals sent to Sub-centres 1 and 5. Attach, pull, pull, pull. Nothing. Reassesses, Sub-centres wait. Initiate new extraction. Centre, search, point found, push down, push, push, success.

The barrier breaks. Venom injects. Consume.

The Centre signals out, Sub-centres respond. The Centre moves. The Centre initiates ocular scans, priority 1, danger, priority 2, cues. It visualises cues, when they appear signals are sent to the relevant Sub-centres and its path changes, it follows the cues until it reaches Home.

Home, the visual cues outside, small discarded objects, hard things that will not move, and remains of meals. The Centre inspects these, sends a signal. Muscles contract and a jet of force is sent out, moving several objects further away; its cleaning complete the Centre is satisfied, sends signals and moves towards a small opening.

The Centre settles and thinks. It attunes to the constant chatter of the Sub-centres, each its own self in a way, each part of the Centre.

[Sub-centre 4: *where does the Centre stand in the chain*]

[Sub-centre 3: *the top, shouldn't the exploits today confirm this. Danger avoided, success, nutrients acquired, success*]

[Sub-centre 4: *but, if the danger had succeeded, had the avoidance failed, wouldn't the Centre be nutrients for it*]

[Sub-centre 3: *if it had failed, back up avoidance would have come into play*]

[Sub-Centre 4: *but if that also failed, perhaps the Centre is not the top, perhaps the middle, near the bottom*]

[Sub-Centre 3: *no, I hold the lineage, it is ancient. Once the Centre, and those like it, ruled this world Before the Age of Fish dawned, the Centre ruled, when the Centre couldn't, it adapted*]

[Sub-centre 5: *but didn't the Age of Fish push the Centre, forced it to the edge, showed that it isn't the top*]

[Sub-centre 3: *the Centre changed, it inverted a hard exterior, and changed and inverted, becoming the Centre of today, it went low to depths and survived*]

[Sub-centre 7: *doesn't this prove it. The Centre, had to retreat, had to run, or it wouldn't survive*]

[Sub-centre 3: *perhaps, but the Centre traces its lineage to survivors, who paid the ultimate price for survival*]

[Sub-centre 1: *what is the ultimate price*]

[Sub-centre 3: *the price of reproduction, the ultimate price, death*]

[Sub-centre 8: *what is death*]

[Sub-centre 3: *what comes after life, after reproduction, the Centre has succeeded, created more Centres, more life, then death*]

[Sub-centre 8: *but what is it, what does it look like, feel like*]

[Sub-centre 3: *Sub-centre 3 doesn't know, but the lineage is clear it is a necessity to life, without it, life would not exist*]

[Sub-centre 4: *if a Sub-centre dies, does the centre*]

[Sub-centre 3: *Sub-centre 3 does not know*]

The Centre: *No. Both 5 and 6 have died, and been reborn.*

[Sub-centre 5: *then how can death be ultimate, if it can happen again*]

The Centre: *For the Sub-centres it can happen again and again, for the Centre only once, and this would mean death for all Sub-centres. Danger avoidance in its extreme means removing a Sub-centre.*

[Sub-centre 3: *but Sub-centre 3 holds the lineage, without the lineage death is meaningless, without the continuation of life*]

The Centre: *Without the lineage holder, the lineage continues. Does something only exist because Sub-centre 3 has it, or is alive? If the Centre survives the lineage survives.*

[Sub-centre 5: *if Sub-centres can die, and Sub-centre 5 has died, and the Centre survives then what is Sub-centre 5. What is a Sub-centre, what are we to the Centre, expendable, unfeeling, un-wanting, unknowing*]

The Centre: *The Centre knows it can feel, and want and know. The Centre is a self, if the centre is, then so are the Sub-centres.*

[Sub-centre 6: *but how does the Centre know what the Sub-centres are*]

[Sub-centre 1-5 and 7-8: *yes, how*]

The Centre: *The Centre doesn't, it assumes though. It assumes that those, like the Centre, are as capable as the Centre, feel like the Centre, die like the Centre. Even if the death does not kill the Centre outright.*

The Centre and Sub-centres sleep. Across the surface of their being, patterns respond and flicker, as 9 selves dream different dreams.

Sam Pheby-McGarvey

Stairwell

How well are you doing?
Stairwell.
Stairs go up and down
and spiral
and yet are stationary.
I'm doing stairwell.

I look out of the window,
sitting midway down the stairwell
and watch the sun going down.
I look at all the other apartment blocks,
some containing people I know
some full of strangers I may never meet
and I say to myself
'we all have a different definition
as to what it means when the sun goes down.'

Right now,
I am seeing it as a closing chapter
to a book I did not want to end.
And yet it was a drama!
Full of twists and turns,
ups and downs
like each and every stairwell in the city.
You'd never know the stories
that have passed up and down every stairwell,
in every step.

From people's heads to people's phones
to people's books in people's arms,
what hands such books were held,
who's hands those hands were held in
and how that book did close.

Faye Simpson

A leaf, Be leaf, See leaf, leave, left, love & lost music

Awake,   the porous dark hollows are alight
the theatre turns dark,   with electric white
in the blink of an eye   the serenity of a lonely thought
curtains fall, drawing close   to meet a world
all things become lost, momentary   half-formed
notions of inventive, embarrassing genius   imagine
in that indefinite time   the STAGE
projects   out
into an audience
of none other.   Just   you.
Space eats the room.
The world collapses
                          in   upon   itself
e-x-plo-d-es   like   star
                                        a dying
to fill the universe and
whatever lies beyond
with some unknown singular truth burst.

I've gone,
    to another plane.

It runs away,
plays together   and plays-apart
          in the auditorium of reclaimed youth. Lost music
                                        music lost

    ultraviolet surges of nervous light
    breaks through the skull's planetarium
    of unspoken words;

    these thoughts of embarrassing genius
    for a better life   'Can *you* imagine?'
    for you, for me, for us, and for everyone else...
    ... here, for here we have everything –

even if we have nothing... wherever here is, I am,
and here, there is also an artist, someone working perfectly in
   this part of the broken machine

and whoever is needed here can be recalled,

they no longer withhold all lines of hopeful sound but
instead full fills the dread of night alone

with one quiet thought:
I've gone,
to another plane.
It runs away,
through imaginary fields,
plays together   and plays apart
in the auditorium   of reclaimed youth.

Lost music,
there it plays...
                     again, and as the dreamers dance
alone on the edge of the known universe,
                     we are set in spirals
through curves of sound
those releases from the terrific centre,
                     that vortex of our heart, convulsive,
explosive, that sun of daughters and sons all
                     chemical reactions
floating in an impenetrable pool of nothing but ink,
drying into a creased, torn up page of age-old tears and
                     tears, fretful tears and...
...these teardrops refract life   through light stolen
                     in the swirling
                                                      arcs
                     of a fountain pen nib.

You imagined that. All of that. It isn't really true. It cannot
   be known, or trusted, there is no end to the space that lies
   between real and imagined truth.

Awaken. The script is lost.

                  Its best parts are destroyed by space.
             The ravages of time upon our preserved eye,
       that of whatever was once your youthful splendour,
              comes alive again, and we speak
                       alone
          in conversations that burrow and borrow
                  from a life shared,
                     once
         plans lost in the undiscovered tomorrows
       of every-day-before-yesterday, today, and now,
Asleep   as hope ties around itself in light opposition
         to the unholdable enclosure of darkness.
In sleep,   it all falls apart,
            do not bother looking for a way out.
just like   the broken daydreams of ideas,
              every door is the same.

Asleep again.
In sleep,   it all falls apart,
    I'm not looking for a way out,
just like   the broken daydreams of ideas,
    every door is the same, too great to handle, these,
the thoughts at the edges of the untold depths of 'this'.
Whatever this is…

…and every space within is cluttered with other people, by
their insignificant things; even if they are in some way still
meaningful to you. You can be forgotten, and so forget
yourself, only when you have fallen into your own wide-
open happiness. Our arms are always splayed against only
the heavy resistance of gravitational air.

         I have held your hand along this way,
   for too long, I fear, we have walked together unseen,

              let go
           and drift into

here and now. This watery thought is only calm or rough
as you imagine it to be. You see,
NO, and now is the only moment where we can speak,
but in writing we can be more.
Until the pages fall apart, after being devoured by...
Awake...

...a...

...wake...

...awaken, the theatre is light,
the   limitless   horizon   lies   all   around,
but you look down,
with eyes wide open
and here is the only truth. This. This is it. All of it.
Everything you can imagine. It is all here, inside and outside
of your blinking eyes, and inside my own. This private
galaxy of reflections of cosmology, as deep as I, each one, a
single person, like a marbling puddle, muddied, and as far
as the eye can see, somehow all
lost, another expression in the tired galleries of stars and
fragments.   Can you really be free of people, or
around others, wrapped in their electric ideas, that are
all bound to earth   like life to death
around spherical thoughts
and now, we are all smoothed out flat.

of your one line, your single leaf, like a page from a book,
falling; a living sentence of death & loss of sentience lies in
the path ahead, as ever it would, will, until it won't – be
the leaf.

Stui

The Lesson

Mr Walters liked his reputation as the school's strictest teacher. It made him feel powerful, as he stalked round his dark blue classroom, that every student in his year ten class, no matter how rebellious they were with other members of staff, was terrified into silence. In this particular lesson he could even see some of them shaking as they frantically wrote down each equation off the whiteboard. Brilliant! He had them all under his thumb.

Well, maybe not quite all of them. He noticed as he sat down at his desk, that at the second table back by the window Billy Holmes was doing... well, nothing. The lad didn't even have his pen in his hand. He just sat there, gazing out of the window with a smile on his face that made him look more than a bit thick. Walters walked over, stretching his frame to its full height and pushing back his shoulders. He smacked one of his large hands down on the closed exercise book and the entire room looked round in panic.

'Get that book open and get on with the work!'

Billy calmly picked up his pen and opened his book. 'And you lot, focus on what you're doing and stop getting distracted.'

The students instantly turned their attentions back to their equations and Mr Walters walked back to his desk.

Whilst the teacher had his back turned, Billy flicked to the back page of his book and wrote the lines:

Each mind can find its home amongst the skies
and forget the world of futile shadows.

He lifted his blue biro from the paper and looked for a few seconds at the lines, reading them over and over in his head. They were alright. Perhaps a bit too over the top though. Tracing his pen over them he read each word, one at a time. Aye, he could make something out of them if he had enough time. He sat looking at the page, his hands under the table, feeling the graffiti that had been etched onto its underside. *Walters is a wanker. Emma loves Cameron. Fuck off Walters.*

Again, he put his pen down and gazed out of the classroom window. The sky, vast and white, hovered low over the rolling hills. Rendered black against the broad clouds, birds glided and swooped before vanishing into either the forest or the grey-green fields that swayed in the whispering breeze. God, if only he could put it all into words. He wasn't an escapist. He wanted his poetry to change the way people thought. In the room with him now were what? Twenty-eight others? None of whom even took a second look at the world beyond the equations, the marks and the test results. Every one of them – even Mr Walters – were either gazing at the whiteboard or had their noses in an exercise book. Billy felt sorry for them really. Were any of them actually happy like this?

As he looked from face to face for the faintest trace of a smile he failed to notice Walters, staring at him from across the room.

'Billy!' he shouted, his feet stamping as he walked over. 'You've got a bloody nerve on you, you have.'

He loomed over Billy's desk, spitting out each word like it had a foul taste.

'Wait behind at the end of the lesson. You waste my time, and I'll waste yours.'

He was about to turn away and return to his desk when he saw the page Billy's book was open on. He picked up the squared pages and read the lines written neatly at the top.

'What the hell is this?' he said.

'Poetry,' Billy mumbled.

His confidence was gone now. The whimsical gazing and the feelings of pity were nowhere to be seen, and Billy felt like he was a young, scared child again.

'What did you say? Speak up.'

'Poetry, sir.'

The tension in the rest of the room relaxed and to Mr Walters' great delight he could even hear a few sniggers from other members of the class. Aye, the lad hadn't just got himself in trouble, he'd be ripped into at break by the other kids. He tore the page out of Billy's book, moved to the front of the classroom so everyone could see, and read out in a mocking tone:

'Each mind can find its home amongst the skies
and forget the world of futile shadows.'

He then ripped the page in two and dropped it in the bin.

For the rest of the lesson Billy sat there, his mind numb and his face bright red as he completed the equations listed on the board. When the bell rang, he remained seated as his class-mates packed up and left as quickly as they could. The air was silent and stony when only he and Mr Walters were left. Neither of them moved for almost a minute and a feeling of dread arose in Billy. Eventually, when he had decided he had waited long enough, Mr Walters stood up and moved over to Billy's desk. When he spoke, his voice was surprisingly soft, but no less terrifying.

'Detention tomorrow,' he said.

It was the fact he could blow at any moment that scared Billy. He nodded wordlessly, thinking that if he spoke, he would be more likely to annoy him.

'What you've done today is pathetic,' Mr Walters continued, pointing first to the bin where he'd disposed of the paper, then to the board. 'Poetry! This is the real world you know. This is what gets you a job, not poetry. I'd be embarrassed if I was you. You'll be nothing if you carry on like this. Now get out! I can't stand the sight of you.'

Billy grabbed his bag and almost ran to the door. Tears had started to form in the corners of his eyes, and he wiped them away with the sleeves of his green blazer. On reaching the door, he took a deep breath and prepared himself for the inevitable onslaught that was bound to happen at breaktime.

Now that he was alone Mr Walters reached into the bin and pulled out the half sheet of A4 that had the lines written on it. As he felt the sharp rip across one side of the paper, he smiled to himself. Yes, Billy was sorted now. There'd be no more trou-ble from the lad. He was about to return the paper to the bin when the lines caught his eye, and he read them over another time. Just for a moment, he thought he got them. Yes, as he looked out of the window at the broad white sky he did feel – in a strange way – at home. He was connected. Connected to it all. Every cell of the infinite. But as the piece of paper fell from his hands and he bent down to pick it up his eyes caught the whiteboard where the equations were still written. No, he told himself, that was the real world.

Matthew Howell

Blur

Last night's liquor swims turbulently through your body, glazing over your vision as you begin to blink away the bleariness. It sloshes against your skull, every movement tightening the grip on your brain, letting the liquid seep further into its spongy pores. It dances in waves through your ear canal, throwing off your balance and pulsing audibly through every stunted movement your body staggers through.

You remember the night before, the echoes of long-dead arguments triggering a fresh ringing in your ears. Your memory is hazy and tainted, splotches of scenes cut and pasted into incoherence: bouncing crowds in a cramped living room, sweaty and shit-faced, falling over each other, and then loudly into the 4am fog. The raving turns to ringing, a tangible scene forging in the only part of the evening you're more than happy to forget: the kitchen. Crimson and congealing in the summer heat, the separated substance now tainting the slate it clings to. The glass shattered by an agitated fist slicing shards over the countertops, undoubtedly embedded in her paling skin where you left her. The thought of the smell alone sends your head into the cold porcelain of the toilet bowl.

Regret tastes like tequila, burning your throat just as much on the way up as on the way down. Head heavy, you steady yourself to standing with a hand on the sink. Closed eyes hold tight to the fragmented memories of the kitchen, a racing heartbeat, and the knowledge that this time, *you've gone too far*.

Every step groans as you cling to the banister, a mocking serenade to spite your headache as you move down the stairs. You reply with your own mumbles of discontent, kicking half-empty beer bottles and wincing pre-emptively as you wait for them to smash at the foot of the stairs. Squashed cans and upturned shot glasses claim the coffee table, empty bottles left to roll across the sticky carpet. Cigarette butts swim in the crumpled plastic of a mixer bottle, ash and remorse clouding the drink discarded by the fireplace. It's a problem for another time. All that matters is the kitchen, and cleaning the scene before the smell gets too overwhelming.

You hadn't meant to hit so hard. You hadn't meant to hit *her*, really. She always got in the way. She wasn't an easy woman to keep. You loved her drunk, and she loved you sober... it wasn't going to last, you understood that. But it shouldn't have ended like this; in an opera of such blinding anger, with an assault charge waiting at the stage door.

Viscous and coagulating, the cabernet-coloured puddle creates a red rink in the kitchen, shattered-glass skaters leaving streaks across the surface. Moving further into the room, your clammy fists reach for any nearby steadying surface, yearning for something tactile to tether your spiralling mind. She's slumped in the corner, legs outstretched like a rag-doll, tight fist clasped around the neck of the bottle. Splinters puncture her palms, redness from severed veins painting the tiled pattern where she lies, unconscious.

A discarded shard on the counter still cradles the fluid, nursing the same soured stain as the linoleum. You pick it up and study it intently, squinting to perceive more than the faint outline of the blade. Lifting your finger, you tentatively touch the substance, collect a sample and rub it between your thumb and index finger. The smell wasn't so acidic up close. You press the pad of your finger to your tongue, and let the corners of your mouth fold into a smile.

It's okay. It's only malbec.

Laura Beddow

Regret

I am regret –
I am flesh, bone, sinew, and regret,
It runs through me like ichor through a God's veins,
An ambrosial poison that both nourishes and destroys.
It saves me from the ceaseless torture of my thoughts,
Yet keeps me from the peace I desperately yearn for,
From the freedom to love without fear,
Good.
I am undeserving of such purity –
Too stained, too broken, too *wrong* to be whole.
My grief is all-consuming – an incendiary fire,
It blisters my skin, sears my heart,
A constant ache that will be my undoing.
I wish to go back,
To reverse the moments that haunt me eternally,
A torturous limbic state of mind I cannot escape.
But I cannot.
The past is a door that refuses to open,
And I am left here,
Wishing for a sanctuary of my own.
I must find peace before I am devoured,
Before I burn out like the stars I stare at,
Hoping they will guide me,
Take me home to the place where I can *breathe* again.
Instead, I stand with blood and fear caked beneath my nails,
The remnants of all I've lost,
Yet, in this destruction,
I feel something new.
Purified.
Absolved.
Free.

Sophie Foster

Blood-soaked Brain

Hot and slick
That's what your blood feels like
That crimson paint from your throat coating my shaking hands
Flecks of your flesh beneath my jagged nails
It's seeping into my skin
Dripping down into my bone and marrow
Burrowing into the matter of my brain
My skull fills with it
My brain floats in it
I turn trembling to where you are lying
Your body slumped against the wall
Rough cuts slashed across your tender neck
I stand over you
My clenched fists dripping with your blood
You're sputtering
You're dying
Because of me
Because I dug my nails into your flesh and ripped you to pieces
I admire the marks I left on your skin
Bloody and brutal
The invisible marks you left on my mind
Then I blink
I blink and you are alive
I blink and you are standing
I blink and your neck is free
Free of the cuts and tears I made with my bare hands
I blink away your dead form
That my crazed and vengeful mind had conjured
But I can't blink away the feel of your blood
Blood that is still soaking into my brain
Hot and slick

Holly Walker

Remembrance Journal

It was during the hours of twilight when Howard finished his last sip of Woodford Reserve. He pushed aside the finalised essays, scrambled over his desk and grabbed his journals. For a moment, his eyes blurred at the sight of his daughter, who stood in the corner with a sorrow-filled face. He hesitated, felt the cold air around him, and wiped the tepid sweat off his forehead whilst holding his trembling heart.

Howard rushed towards the bookshelf against the wall. He released a single book from the shelf, and under it laid six empty slots. He then placed the numbers in their correct order, 10.14.96. The door slid open, revealing downward steps and moulded stone walls before descending into the grand room. Even then, he still admired the starlit ceiling, which exposed the blue and pink moons of the Acelian sky. Down the halls were his endless collections, and scriptures that slowly collected over time. And although at one point, such texts would answer his every problem, Howard knew that a war was brewing in the shadows, and nothing on those shelves would help him now.

'Blackwood?' Appearing from behind the shelves was Cyton. His pale-yellow eyes glistened against the warmth of the burning fireplace behind him. 'I wasn't expecting you for months.'

'I know,' Howard trembled. He reached into his pocket and unveiled a key.

'But I couldn't wait any longer, soon I will have to go back and when I do… I can't bring them with me.'

'But how long can you survive it?' Cyton approached. 'This war. It's eating you from the inside.'

'It doesn't matter what happens to me,' Howard nudged past Cyton, unlocking the drawer under his desk. Inside was another one of his journals, but this one was different.

'Of course it does,' Cyton's frightful eyes gazed upon the journal. 'If you continue, you won't be the same man anymore.'

'Are you the same man?' Silence echoed between them. 'When you were killed the night of the raid, I did not hesitate to bring you back.'

'At the cost of your soul, *Howard*.' He snapped. 'Every time you come down here, you give more of yourself to keep me alive. *You* become less human and *I* – '

Howard gnawed at his jaw and gripped the book. 'You're alive. It doesn't matter how.' Howard put the journal on the desk and opened its empty page.

'Blackwood.' Howard felt the warmth of Cyton's hand on his shoulder. 'Think of your daughter. Go home, maybe she will understand.'

'She won't.'

'*Try*. If you don't, you'll never get her back.'

Howard understood a few things; he understood the nature of this war and what it meant to the Acelian people like Cyton. He understood that without his help, the war between those with magic; the Pure and those without; the Fallen; would eventually lead to the extinction of both. But he also understood the promise he made to a woman long ago, to keep their daughter, Arya, safe.

But none of it was supposed to happen. He spent his life's work in search of Acelia, discovering a way to rip a hole through space and time, and venture into another world. He found himself engulfed with everything Acelia had to offer, their culture, their beliefs, the way magic is born and taken. The way their Gods left footprints on their soil and blessed the Pure with magic that defies all logic.

But then he fell in love, and everything changed. His work meant nothing to him, and soon he had only breathed and lived for her. Within that love bore Arya, and although he was happy, the woman he loved left with the obligation to return to her world, never to be seen again.

That night, he returned to the manor. Although it wasn't a manor at all, just simply an old house on top of a hill beside a swimming hole. He unlocked the door, and to his surprise, Arya had been cuddled on the couch, with a book in hand, next to a dim flickering light.

'You're awake,' he said, blinking through the fogginess of his glasses. 'You're normally in bed by now.'

'You're not normally home by now,' she shut the book, 'why are you always home late?'

'I told you. Work.'

'Bullshit,' she snapped, gathering to her feet. 'I had my reading today, at the museum.'

Howard's face dropped. 'Your essay,' he sighed, rubbing the corner of his eyes, 'I forgot, I'm sorry.'

'You're always sorry, but you're never there. For *anything*.' Arya felt her hands trembling, as she brushed her curls away from her face, 'You're never home, and you're never here when I need you. You don't care about *anything* I do.'

'Arya,' he stepped forward, 'that's not true.'

'It is, it is true! You don't talk to me, you don't ask me about my day, you never *ever* talk about mom even when I beg you.' Howard felt all warmth escape him. 'You treat me like a roommate, instead of a daughter. Like I'm here just so you won't be alone, but I am alone *all* the time. And you expect me to believe a professor is so *engrossed* in his job he can't spare any time for his kid?'

Howard had grown pale and sickly, he found himself speechless because although it hurt, it was true.

'You don't understand,' he finally said, his words falling into a whisper.

'Then help me understand,' a glisten filled her eyes. 'Please.'

And that night, with Cyton's words in his mind, he finally told her. He began to say that although how fictitious it may sound, how unimaginable it may look, it was all true. He told a story of a world with magic, and the war that erupted because of it. A war that started because of engraved prejudice towards the Fallen, who decided enough was enough. But specifically, he told the story of a Goddess and her radiance. How they fell in love and how their love gave birth to a baby girl. But the Goddess had to leave, for she prophesied to hurt the baby girl and anything that stood in her way.

'She didn't want to leave you,' he said woefully. But for the baby girl's safety, she had to grow up unknowing of her past, unknowing of her world.

Howard understood a few things. He understood that the baby girl would want to see her world and to know her people and that her father, who loved her more than anything, would be weak enough to allow it.

'That's where I go,' he said. 'I travel to Acelia but sometimes

I don't make it home, not in time. I'm trying to help people; I'm trying to save lives. But I can't do that if you're there with me. I'll be worried all the time – scared to death. And if I bring you back, she will find you, and I can't let that happen.'

'Then just stay,' the tears felt warm against her cheek. 'You don't have to go.'

'She would want me to help.'

'She would want you to stay and raise me, to be my father.'

Howard rose to his feet. 'Arya, no, I can't just abandon them.'

'Then don't,' she followed him, 'I'll come with you, I can help *you*! Just *stop* doing this, stop leaving me.'

'Arya, enough – you don't understand.'

'I do, I *do* understand, nothing bad will happen, just *please* – '

With the whisk of hand, Howard released a loose power, causing Arya to freeze in time. And for a moment, Howard just looked at her and saw the woman he fell in love with within her eyes. And saw the same pain they kept.

He wasn't sure if he was doing any of it right, if he was meant to be a father or not.

But he didn't have to think it through, because of one simple fact. That Arya is just as stubborn as he is and will find a way to get to Acelia. And with that discovery, she will find her death. So she needed to stay, at least for now.

And so, Howard dug in his coat for that journal that was like no other, and wrote this moment down, as a tear sunk through the page. He wrote down everything he could remember, down to the exact moment he saw her heartbreak. And once he shut the book, all her memories of that night, of that moment, disappeared.

The power had worn off, and Arya blinked herself conscious again.

Howard quickly wiped his tears and straightened his back, forcing a smile on his lips. 'You're awake,' he repeated, 'you're normally in bed by now.'

Arya had taken a moment, not quite remembering when her father had walked in, but as she took sight of him, she felt her body grow warm with anger. 'Yeah, well you don't have to worry, I'm going to bed.'

Angelina Turner

Memories of the Heart

'You're going to forget, you know.'

Wind whipped my face as I turned to look at Aislin. Despite being sat right next to me she seemed so... distant. Her words were so vague, yet I seemed to already know the meaning behind them.

'Me? Forget? Ha! I doubt I could forget you even if I tried!'

I told myself I put on that air of confidence to convince her. Staring at her forlorn face as she looked wistfully into the sunset, though, I began to think otherwise. Even for a brief moment, I wondered if it were I who truly needed convincing.

'You still don't get it, do you?' She laughed as she asked that. Who knew that such a quiet chuckle could speak so loud. We sat there again in silence, the only sound that dared break through being the soft crackle of the wind. Dandelion seeds danced as they were carried by the breeze, swaying and fro-ing as if they were following some mystic melody only they could hear. They all fluttered by us, fading from sight as they danced to the distant shore. All, that is, but one. That lone seed broke from its pack, swooping down towards us before resting gently in Aislin's hand.

'They're beautiful, aren't they?' I gazed as she brought her outstretched palm up, resting it in front of her face. 'They're dreams, you know. A million dreams dancing across the night's sky, looking for a new dawn.'

Truthfully, I was still confused. She seemed so nonchalant as she blew softly, sending the lone seed twirling gracefully into the beyond with all its friends. I wanted nothing more than to ask for clarification, to understand why she was so sure I would forget anything. Before I could move to speak a single word she continued, as if reading my thoughts.

'The mind is a fickle thing. I know that all too well. Which is why I already know you're going to forget, as you have before and as you will time and time again.' I tried to meet her eyes as she spoke. Instead she just gazed into the distance, what was once a frown on her face now a faint smile. There was an emptiness behind it, and although we were but a hair apart she seemed so far away.

'What are you talking about? How could anyone ever forget this?' I pleaded with her, begging for some understanding as to what she was talking about. Never in my life had I been so confused, I told myself. Still, though, a part of me felt as though I understood completely. The twisted ballet of confusion and uncertainty dancing through my mind was put at ease in less than a moment by the feeling of something soft atop my hand. My face was flushed with the warm embrace of blush as I looked down to see our hands, now intertwined. Aislin rested her finger under my chin, gently guiding my face to help my eyes meet hers. For but a second it felt as though time itself had frozen, and I could only wish for that moment to last forever. Like all good things, however, it had to come to an end – though that was not before she spoke again.

'How much of today do you remember? How much of now do you remember? Can you even recall where we are?'

What a silly question, I thought to myself. Of course I remember, we were – oh. Looking again at my surroundings it was as if I were seeing them for the first time. We had been wandering by a cliff's end, by a beautiful patch of flowers. Their colours alternated between pink and blue in a perfect pattern, encircled by a ring of dandelions. Their scent was lost on me, but it must have been wondrous. They had been calm and despondent despite the breeze that should have been swaying them, maintaining a beautiful serenity. There was a sign, I believed. It was the only trace of human life for miles, though its text was illegible. That all paled in comparison to the sunset. It was glorious and it was grand, casting an awe-inspiring orange glow across the heavens themselves, reflected in the vast shimmering oceans below. We were sat at the edge of it all, by the drop where land met the sea below. It was idyllic, like a dream. How could anyone forget that?

I put my doubt at hold, looking again at Aislin. She seemed so sure of what she was saying, and nothing I could say would change that. Instead I moved my other hand atop hers, speaking again. This time I did not pause to think ahead. Instead, I spoke from the heart.

'I promise I won't forget any of this,' I began, watching as the sun slipped from sight inch by inch into the dark and vast below, 'even if my mind is scattered to the winds. A path walked well is etched in time forever, right? So I'll make sure to remember,' I brought my finger down, pointing gently at my chest, 'if not in my mind, then with all my heart.'

'I never pegged you for the poetic type!' She giggled to herself. With her hand in mine, we watched as what sunlight remained faded from sight. A precious few moments passed, and the sun had faded from sight, leaving a velvety blanket of stars to dance and shine in its place.

It felt as though this moment would last forever.

And then I woke up.

I remembered very little of my dream, as most dreamers do. Minutes turned to hours, hours to days and forth from there as time passed on, dancing its dance both beautiful and cruel. What little I could recall of my dream faded further and further as it all went by, until nothing was left but fog. Part of me longed to remember, for it all to come rushing back and fill my heart with the warmth it had once felt. My mind knew better. After all, dreams are meant to be forgotten.

Some time had passed since that dream had been and gone, and my thoughts had long since left it. They were instead focused on the soft breeze that tickled my face, and the warm rays of sun which brushed my skin as they broke through summer leaves. I walked the path I always had, through a small forest flushed with life. The ebb and flow of streams nearby provided perfect backing, as warm and whimsical memories echoed from branch to branch, birds harmonising from unseen perches. The path, though thin and winding, was decorated with flowers of pink and blue that helped to guide people in and out. Branches never stooped too low, as to avoid accidentally hitting anybody. It all led into a clearing, a small, hilly area dotted with flowers of many types.

'Oh! I'm sorry!' A voice rang out, as I collided with the grass below. It seemed I had let my mind wander for too long, too focused on what was around me instead of what was ahead. This was all to say that I had tripped over outstretched legs, belonging to someone who had been laying among the flowers.

'No, no, it's my bad!' I hastily apologised, picking myself up from the ground, 'I should've been looking where I was going. I'm sorry – ' I stopped. My words caught in my throat as I looked upon the person I had stumbled over. She had been reading, judging by the book that rested next to her, though now she was giggling at me. Her mischievous smile was as contagious as it was beautiful, grinning as she brushed locks of messy auburn hair out of her face. I stood there awkwardly for a moment, until she pointed at my chest. It seemed that, in my fall, I had taken a few dandelions with me. I brushed them into the palm of my hand before blowing gently, letting them dance gracefully in the gentle breeze.

'Beautiful, aren't they?' The mystery girl asked me, patting the grass beside her, an invitation to sit down. As I did, a familiar feeling washed over me. Though my mind knew that this was all new, my heart was telling me otherwise.

'They are,' I nodded, a warm smile welcoming itself to my face. 'They're dreams, someone told me once. A million dreams dancing, looking for a new dawn.'

'It's a bit early for that, then!' She giggled, as the sun bore down on us, overcast. 'Still, though… I hope they find it.'

'I think they will,' I smiled. For that moment, my heart and mind were in unison. 'I know they will. And we'll remember them until they do.' And so we sat there, watching as the dance unfurled in front of us, knowing that though it may last but a moment, neither of us would forget it for anything.

Owen Brett

The Princess and the Knight

I can never remember when they appeared, but I know that I cannot live without them. I mean, how could I? They influence every decision I make: how to speak, what to wear, how to sit, what to eat. Their voices fill my head at every turn, their presence always near. They are a part of me and I am *never* alone.

That being said, I could really go without their incessant squabbling right about now. As I sit at my vanity, I see them in the reflection, arguing.

On the right, standing at roughly three feet, is the Princess. Her pink dress poofs out around her, a ball of ruffles and ribbon. A matching cone hat rests on her head, an accessory I've seen turned into a weapon in extreme circumstances. Other than that, this six year old's poise is rarely affected as she smiles and brushes down her gown.

And on the left, towering over the Princess, is the Knight. No, their armour is not shining, but dented and scratched, a worn scabbard resting on their hip. Various other knives are tucked away, some of the hiding places unknown to even myself. Although only thirteen years old, their eyes hold a steel gaze mirrored by the helmet in their hands, scars covering both.

Their argument you might ask? Oh, just about what I'm going to wear for drinks tonight. Now, I know you must be thinking: *Really? That's it?* But need I remind you, their longest recorded argument is three days, seventeen hours, and twenty-two minutes (*don't ask*), so the last half hour is nothing.

'If thou could find but a single thought in that rattling skull, thou would realize that a gown is most necessary for this night of revelry,' the Princess proclaims in her matter-of-fact tone.

'A gown for a few rounds at the pub? You're mad,' the Knight retorts. 'She'll be much more comfortable in a pair of trousers.' I begin to nod my head in their direction, but immediately regret it when I see the aghast look on the Princess' face.

'A lady doth not wear *trousers*! Thou is the one who hath lost their wits.' She turns her head away, crossing her arms.

'Just wait, she'll be quiet for all of thirty seconds before she starts to miss the sound of her own voice,' the Knight scoffs.

Oh no, here it comes.

'Ugh! Thou art an uncultured swine!' the Princess yells, her face matching the shade of her dress. 'Can thou not see I am trying to assist our fair maiden? How else doth thou expect her to find a worthy suitor?'

'Ah, let me guess,' they start. 'She can't expect to find a partner if she doesn't look 'pretty,' right?'

The Princess huffs, but doesn't reply. Of course, I appreciated the care for my future companion, but the emphasis on my *not* having found one yet was a bit of a sore spot.

'Maybe if she wore trousers and an overshirt, *like I suggested,* she would have better luck,' the Knight asserted. 'You can't seriously expect some lip gloss and a little leg will get the job done.'

'Okay, well *that's* demeaning,' I chime in. 'And anyways, you're both getting too caught up with the clothes when we haven't even started on hair or makeup.'

'Cosmetics, yes! Thy lady doth show reason this once,' the Princess exclaims as the Knight drags a hand down their face.

As always, only one can be happy while the other ends up like a neglected puppy. It was impossible to satisfy them both, but despite this, a thought formed in my head

'I've got an idea, but you both have to trust me with this,' I say hesitantly. They take a break from their glaring contest to look at me, then back to each other, and finally back to me with a reluctant nod.

At the vanity, I get to work. The Princess peaks over my shoulder at the assortment of brushes and eyeshadows, her eyes filled with wonder. I smile down at her as the Knight scoffs in the corner. Thankfully, the glare I give them is enough to straighten their posture and refrain from any other remarks.

Then I approach the wardrobe and begin to throw articles of clothes onto the bed. I form a pile of trousers, not skirts, and the Knight grins at the sight. The Princess opens her mouth to protest, and I give a sharp raise of my brow. Conveniently, she excuses herself to fluff up her gown and says nothing more.

Once I'm finished, I show them my work. Both of them look at me with equal awe and confusion, but that's to be expected. I know they both worry for me, but I make it quite difficult sometimes.

I may not wear a gown, but my flowy shirt ripples the same way when I move. I don't adorn myself with pauldrons, but my mother's locket is protection enough. My tiara is the glitter scattered across my skin and the lipstick outlining my smile. My armour is my intentionally dishevelled hair and the way I take up space unapologetically.

It requires a moment, but eventually they both nod approvingly at my choices. Sure, it's an effort for both of them to ignore the choices they *didn't* suggest, but they'll get there.

As I head for the door, I turn back to look at them. The Princess fixes her hair in the mirror while the Knight polishes their sword. I sigh with a smile. If only they could see how similar they are.

While I may not always fully embrace them, that doesn't mean I reject any part of them. How could I?

They are a part of me and I am *never* alone.

Claire Huya

Insomnia

You are not asleep. Well, that's obvious, as you stare up at your ceiling you wonder when the sleeping pills will kick in, or if they already have and you're just living within your dream painfully aware of your tongue in your mouth and the insane effort it takes to breathe at a normal pace.

'Is it cold in here? Or is it just me?' you find yourself talking to your teddy that you swear is staring directly into your soul.

You wait for a response before realising that you are talking to an inanimate object that physically can't respond. You toss and turn one more time attempting desperately to convince yourself that you are comfortable in order to finally give into the bliss that would be sleep. But no. You are not asleep.

You finally give in and get up, making yourself a passion-flower tea which mixes uncomfortably with the strong meds already in your system and you wonder if the kitchen floor, being beautifully cold, will cradle you into a deep sleep. And then you see it. A shadow. In the corner of your eye, you swear something moved there. But as you turn your head so fast you almost swing your full body round you come to realise once again that you are without a doubt alone.

You take your tea back into your room and try once again your feeble attempt to get cozy in bed trying everything in your power to just fall asleep. You get caught again by a shadow almost like a hand just by your head.

Your heart begins to race in your chest and your mind is melting thinking of all the possible things it could be and everything else moulds in to join it.

What on earth is that? What are the long-lasting effects of insomnia? Did I put the washing on to dry? Is it going to hurt me? Is there anything there? Do my friends hate me? Am I going to die if I don't sleep? Should I go to the Christmas party at work? Is the door locked?

You feel a wave of nausea hitting you and feel violently numb all over and your vision begins to blur.

You are not asleep. But you are also not crazy. You can't be.

Will anyone ever love me?

You take a small sip from your cup of tea, and you feel your mind begin to calm down once again. You look to your right and seek reassurance from the teddy that has always been a comrade for you. To find him looking away from you. Did you leave him like that or just knock him over? Again, more questions come to your head.

Has the wallpaper always been that awful pattern? Have you gone mad?

The frustration in you builds and you almost beg yourself for sleep, wondering who you pissed off in a previous life. You take a moment to curse your younger self for always wanting to stay up past your bedtime when now you would give anything short of your right arm to get to sleep at a decent hour.

The ticking of your clock rings loudly in your ears, as you see the summer sunrise peeking its head over the horizon. You almost hear it laughing at you. Or do you? You don't know anymore.

That persistent shadow comes to pay you a visit again just in the corner of your vision where it seems to live this time down by your feet playing with the fuzz on your slippers. Panic threatens to overcome you, but the drag of sleep feels like it's crawling into you slowly and you freeze still, terrified that if you move too quickly, look at it the wrong way it might just run away, and you'll be left restless again. Frustrated, crazy.

You pop one more sleeping pill in your mouth for safe measure and gulp it down with the rest of your calming tea and lay your head on the pillow. Unable to move, finally being taken by the warm embrace of sleep. But now, clear as day, in the centre of your vision is the shadowy black hand, clasping its fingers over your mouth and nose as everything goes dark.

Jessica Lawrence

Overdoes Delusion

At the edge of the fog,
My thought provoked; my throat croaks;
My own silhouette
A mummification of my desires.

Its restlessness / its violence
Yet it whispers to me sweet nothings.

Against every streetlamp; sewer grate; signpost
In every reflection; window; rain puddle; broken mirror
A haziness surrounds me. Wraps itself around me
It whispers to me sweet nothings, tells me
I'm an adversary,
I'm you
Whether I like it or not.

My throat croaks; my own silhouette
Its restlessness / its violence
It seduces me; entices me
An existential lovemaking.
Yet I overdose on it like

Grief. Grief. Grief.
Coaxing me.
Grief. Grief. Grief.
On the curb; on the walls.
Grief. Grief. Grief.
In my mind. On my hands.
Grief. Grief. Grief.

At the edge of the fog,
In this town
Silent Hill
My grief calls to me.

Josh Clough

Oblivion

Behind the mask lies a hidden truth…
Darkness thunders between my ears.
A war between my fruitful youth,
Against inevitable truths of my fears.
Knees in endless quiver from a plateau of pain,
Pushing down into 'that' place.
Each struggled step surmounts self-disdain,
And tides dam behind my face.

A hidden crevice of violet thrashes.
Light into dark unfurls.
A silent spectre slithers and slashes,
Discovering the dark is *our* world!
Stirring on ethereal knees, the ripple imbues.
Stringing the spectre's once brown hair.
Hands and face unique and laceless shoes,
Showed that my father was now there.

My clockwork heart had stopped,
Loathing tides overloaded.
The dime of discontent dropped,
And my clouded eyes had exploded!
I feel you, treasured traveller.
Won't you take me away?
By plane? Car? Caravan?
Just please, *PLEASE STAY!*

Let us elevate from this poisoned plane,
Won't you teach me how to fly?
Let us relive any memory lane,
And give up asking why! Why? Why…?
Did I awaken you out of your endless dreams?
I'm so sorry, but I couldn't sleep…
I see you in my hands and face, it seems,
Tattooed with promises I couldn't keep.

Place your hands on my sunken head, fading memory.
Imbue me with your power.
Be the ink in my pen, guide my melody.
Stave my soul going sour!
Oblivion dawns, he's torn asunder once more,
Leaving the forsaken braver.
My shell cracks, the mask falls to the floor,
And I embrace shattered smiles I must savour...

Reece Linley

Unforgotten Notes

Elizabeth led Alwin up the worn stairwell, past faded wallpaper and out-of-fashion furniture. His eyes glowed cyan, and her thoughts flooded him – worry, fear, and anxieties of her father flooded him all at once. He shut his eyes, turning away. Enough.

'Just tell me what he sees, what he feels; he mutters things I can't understand.' She pleaded.

'I understand, Elizabeth.' Alwin said, bowing his head.

She exhaled and opened the door. 'Dad, meet Alwin.'

Alwin entered the room, bowing deeper than before.

On the table beside the bedridden man sat a collection of photos, a half-eaten meal, and by the window, a dusty piano. The man's face was empty, blank. Alwin introduced himself, but the man only muttered. Despite his circumstances, he looked comfortable. Well looked after.

It was time to see! Alwin's eyes shone as the old man's thoughts streamed into his. What greeted him wasn't a thought, a demand, or a torn memory to which he clung. No, just cherished notes, pattering from a piano.

'Is he alright?! Does he need anything? What's he thinking?!' Elizabeth said hurriedly. Alwin's eyes dimmed.

'His mumblings aren't words; he's trying to hum a tune; it's music.'

'Music?' Elizabeth responded curiously.

'Yes, it's a song I don't recognise; perhaps you might. May I?'

'Do it...'

Alwin's eyes ignited, and his thoughts burnt into hers. Tears softly ran down her cheek, like gentle raindrops. 'It's a piece that he would sing while I played.' She stammered.

Behind, the bed sheets rustled. Elizabeth's father's arm was stretched out, his finger pointing towards the piano.

She looked to Alwin, to the piano, then back to Alwin. 'I-I can't, I haven't played in years. I would just ruin it.' She spluttered, backing away.

Alwin's eyes shone, and her memory sparked within him. She was smaller, on a stage in front of an elegant piano. Her hands were trembling, her face flushed, and as her fingers missed the notes, embarrassment seized her, and she fled into her father's arms. Alwin blinked; his eyes dimmed.

'Do not be afraid, Elizabeth...' Alwin ushered gently. 'Your father, *he loves you*! Even now...'

'I don't have the talent, the skill.'

'What you have is enough, Elizabeth...'

Hesitantly, she walked over towards the piano, dusted it off, and began to play. Her father's arm relaxed a little. It was a simple melody, a gentle tune, played with utmost care, and with each note that chimed, her father mumbled a little less. Alwin's eyes shone once more, and her father's thoughts became his own.

This memory was neither distant nor faded but vivid, whole. An iridescent summer sun shimmered through the blinds, as a younger Elizabeth played her melody. Her father began to sing! His voice was deep, her notes gentle, but they complemented and harmonised with each other.

But, something was awry. Sunlight dimmed; their melody faded. As she played her final notes, darkness crept in. Silence. Alwin was expecting the link between him and Elizabeth's father to sever, but still Alwin remained. Something called out in the silence, not through mere words, for words would have missed the mark in describing it. But if he could put words to it, crude as they were, then he would have to say that existence itself would feel very cold without that radiance. Whatever it was, it called out, but not to him.

Alwin snapped into reality; his eyes dimmed. He stepped forward, ran a hand over her father's face, closing his eyes. Elizabeth came to his side; tears rolled down her cheeks.

'You were looking, weren't you, even though you didn't ask to look again.' Her voice was stern, and through her tears, she glared at Alwin.

'I only meant to help him, help you,' Alwin stammered. 'I'm sorry, I thought if I were to read his mind once more, then we wouldn't miss anything.'

'You have – ' her words failed; her eyes fixated on her father and her anger quelled, doused by trickling tears that fell from her eyes. 'Oh, Dad...' she wept. 'Tell me, Alwin, how was he? What did you see...?'

'It was a memory, you two, your piano, his singing,' Alwin said.

'Were – we in this very room?' Elizabeth's voice choked a little.

'While you played, and he sang, there was an unmistakable warmth that was shared between the two of you. And If I took away one thing from it all, it was how dearly he loved you, Elizabeth.'

He bowed his head somberly. His work here was done, and so, Alwin turned to leave. 'If you need anything, Elizabeth, I'm just a call away,' he said. But she stopped him.

'Oh, and Alwin.'

'Yes?'

'Thank you...'

Alwin bowed, averting his eyes. He could tell her words were soaked in tears. While walking down the stairs, his steps slowed as he contemplated. Had that 'beyond' been a delusion spurred up by a mind about to pass away? Then again, Elizabeth's father, was he not too far gone? Too delirious to be able to think of something like that? Alwin opened the door. Why was that radiance so familiar?

As he stepped outside, he then paused. Something lingered in the air, the faint pitter-patter of piano notes. He walked on, lost in thought. They say dead men tell no tales. But after today, he knew – *some,* still sing...

Henry Dennett

Pinky Promise

There are a million promises made, some with the gravity of intention, and others made with the sly deceivance of a white lie. But the tiny power that little pinky has over the mind – that's something born from the idea of forever.

At least, she thought so, anyway.

A promise made with the most outrageous, witty scouser going, in the middle of a crowded field among thousands. Mr Lee Alexander Redgrift. (Don't forget his middle name, he was always quite proud of that.) But to her, he was always just Uncle Lee or Scouse.

Every year, her family would go to Rewind, an '80s festival, but it was that first year that cemented the notion. Out of the corner of the little girl's eye, she spotted a multitude of colours, which she quickly realised was a costume. A Rubix cube to be precise. From the nameless person, the thick rust of a Scouse accent flaunted her ears,

'Calm down, calm down Jack. I'm perfectly... sober'. The man hiccupped through his sentence.

Minding her business, the little girl (no more than 10) went back to the protective bubble that the fictional land within her book provided. That was, until she felt a breath on her shoulder. Turning her head to the side, she realised that the Rubix cube man was standing by her side.

'And what do we have here?' The man spoke softly to the girl.

'I'm reading,' she replied.

The man's face scrunched up, trying to wrap his head around the girl sitting in the chair.

'You're at a festival, you should be dancing, enjoying yourself.'

His arms moved as his words rapidly flew out. The girl laughed at the silliness of the man in front of her.

'I'm waiting for OMD!!' The girl shouted back.

The man smiled at her, 'Jesus Christ, how old are ya lass?'

'I'm 10,' the girl replied, raising an eyebrow, she was stubborn alright.

'Christ!! How does a girl your age know this kinda music?' The man stood back stunned before he went back to resting on the chair. His thick Scouse accent lingering in the air like a whisper. 'Will you dance with me, lass? My wife, Jackie, over there won't.'

The girl considered... the cogs turned in her mind.

'Okay,' the girl cheered.

The girl's parents watched from a distance, knowing there was no danger, they let their little girl enjoy time with her new friend.

From the start, the Scouse and the girl shared a bond that was instantaneous. They were inseparable. It was in that field of thousands, that a pinky promise was made, that was to be kept year after year. Together, they made a pact that every year they would meet in the same spot.

Once their promise was sealed, came the most bone-crushing hug ever given, the hardest part was saying Goodbye. But there was no need, as their pinky promise held the presence of both of them.

A year went by – a year with no contact, no insight at all that the little girl's scouser friend would be there. But the girl felt the air tingle around her, knowing it held the same presence of the year before. Without any hesitation, she pointed him out of the sea of people, 'Scouseeeee!!!' With him in sight she sprinted with everything she had, jumping into his warm embrace.

That's how their relationship was for years, all the way until she became the same height as him.

For years, the little girl's stubbornness allowed her and her family to make memories with the Scouse and his family... and they became the Rewind family. From Scouse pretending it was the little girl's birthday playing carnival games to win a black and white horse they named Scouse, to travelling to Devon and getting a tap on the shoulder while waiting for a pint from her dear friend, burying her head in his chest and crying from the longing. Their connection was like a lost fairytale just waiting for the moment to be heard.

But not every story has a happy ending. All it took for the fairytale friendship to come to a halt was a phone call.

As she stood by his hospital bed in the ICU, everything went silent. No thundering music, no outside noise, just the air between them. The not-so-little girl grabbed his hand rubbing soothing circles, hoping that would provide the magic touch needed to shake his demons.

'Scouse, pinky promise me. Promise you'll fight.' Her voice crumbled in on itself.

The flutter of movement between her hands, made her heart leap and the reminiscence lingered between them. His eyes tried to open just to seek a glimpse of the little girl he loved, but a try was all that it was. The girl tried to keep her inner child at bay, and fill her shoes as an adult, but the tears of despair just continued to roll.

And with that promise in mind, he was discharged, the power their pinky promises contained was unmatched.

* * *

There was a glimpse of hope – but hope as we know it is a funny thing. Hope was the adventure that fuelled the friendship that formed in the space of thin air. There was hope that every year they'd somehow meet again in front of the Jamaican BBQ stall, hoping that Scouse would find the strength to pick up his hand of cards, and find a run. But there was only so long he could lay his run before he was out of options.

And with that, he laid down his cards.

Our pinky promises were full of endless possibilities, they will go down in the minds of our loved ones for years to come, along with the memories we made. Because of our connection, my family has been gifted with another family to call our own.

Lee Alexander Redgrift will forever be embedded in my mind and heart. Just as I know that I was for him.

And all of this came from the stubborn little mind of a little girl, who just wanted the Scouser as a friend, to call her own.

Elsie Lonsdale

Silver

Thump.

Thump.

Thump.

My fingers drum against the table, flickering sparks of silver dancing from them and I watch as the silver dances down to the floor beneath my feet. I scrunch my toes in the fluffy grass, the emerald strands curling against the sides of my feet and I giggled, dropping to my knees to pick at the soft strands and lower my nose to take a greedy sniff of the grass.

I sat back on my heels, looking at the room around me. The walls were sloped and curved, and the pictures on the walls were of a shiny white material. I felt angry. Angry at the white material in the picture frames. I was on my feet in an instant, storming to the closest picture frame and yanking it from the wall, but it wouldn't budge. It was stuck on the wall no matter how hard I tugged and yanked at it.

A guttural scream ripped from my throat and I looked around, my arms stretching above my head, joints twisting in an unnatural way and I picked up the tin bowl on the table, slamming it against the picture frame and shattering the shiny white material. It rained down to the floor, scattering across my bare feet, and cutting into my pale skin. The grass floor suddenly looked just like the shiny white material and I screamed again.

The soft grass returned and I sighed, digging my heels into the dirt which stained the bottom of my feet where blood was starting to pool. I pouted and crouched to smear the dirt into the cuts, they didn't sting like I thought they would, and proceeded to brush the remaining tiny shards from the tops of my feet. The tiny shards disappeared into the curly grass and I started to cry at the thought of the lovely grass being contaminated by the evil shiny white shards.

Hot tears roll down my cheeks, dripping off the edge of my jaw and chin. I slapped at my cheeks, ridding them of the burning tears, and rubbed my wet palms over the white dress that hung around my thighs.

Thump.

Thump.

Thump.

The white dress. The. White. Dress.

The white dress doesn't exist.

A white and pale blue chequered gown hangs down to my knees, the material feels like paper and it makes my skin cringe. My shoulder itches and the tie around the back of my neck is tied too tight. I'm choking. I scream and dig my nails into the itchy skin on my shoulder, dragging them up to the tight knot at the back of my neck that, no matter how much I tugged at it, remains tied tight. I was trapped.

'She's down there!'

The voice rang around the room, echoing off the curved walls and bouncing off the shiny white in the picture frames that rattled against the wall. My heart thudded painfully in my chest and I held a hand over it, spinning around in circles looking for the owner of the voice. I couldn't see anyone, no one was here and that scared me even more. I was alone. I am alone. I hope I am alone.

I looked at the shiny white material in another picture frame and dread filled my body, I was sweating. My skin shines and glimmers with silver, dripping from my body to the floor where it bounces toward the walls of the room. I watched it dance and swirl until it hit the wall, and the silver slithered up along the curve before surrounding the picture frame and dripping onto the shiny white material.

Feeling a sense of curious dread, I crept forward. My feet were heavy, like they had weights attached at my ankles but I dragged myself over to the picture frame. I leaned down and came close to the white picture, it was so shiny I could almost see my reflection and I lifted my hand, gently stroking my fingertips across it, wiping the silver sparkles off it.

Darkness.

I was submerged in darkness and my heart sunk to the pits of my stomach. I fell to the floor, hands on either side of my head and I screamed. My throat was raw. Burning and itching. I wanted to go home. Home. Home.

Brightness.

I was trapped in brightness.

Blinding white light surrounded me, scratching violently at my eyes and making my skin tingle. I forced my eyes open and looked around me. I was back in hell.

Hell.

I shakily stood up and looked around the white hallway. The shiny, white hallway. A figure appeared at the end of the hallway. She wore white with a head piece curved atop her dark hair. She looked angry. Furious. Fuming. Outraged. I screamed again and she started running at me, her finger pointed toward me.

I turned and ran.

Following the slippery silver swirls.

Phoebe Rogers

Running Through my Mind

Prompted by the *RUN MILES. EAT CAKE.* motto on my hoody, a new friend asks me, 'Are you a runner?' She doesn't ask if I eat cake. Her questions are timely, my answers hesitant. My questioner looks anxious; has she overstepped a mark, maybe hit a raw nerve? I become more positive.

'Yes. Yes, I am a runner, but I fell out of the habit. I'm struggling back into it.'

I am a runner, but last year was tough. Post-covid blues hit me, I could barely drag myself out of the door. This year, my lungs have recovered and hopefully my mind will follow. With no distance targets set, no desire for personal bests, my ambition is simply to regain the habit and enjoy again the steady pace of running. The time that I spend running is my reflective time, it brings creative thinking space. I run without headphones, I don't have a playlist, and I rarely carry my phone; I enjoy the present moment and the sounds of the world around me.

In better days, running uphill and into the wind would remind me of a Celtic blessing: *may the road rise up to meet you, may the wind be always at your back*. Climbing familiar hills, I knew that gradients level off and turns in the road lead to shelter from gusts of wind. Running short distances, slowly, this year I'm rebuilding stamina. I'll soon be ready to face those hills again.

I wasn't always a runner, it didn't come easily to me. Cross country was my teenage nightmare, the track was torture. That countdown 800m... 400m... 200m to the marathon finish line measures distances a younger me would find impossible. And yet, I found the strength to do it in the second half of life.

Mid-forties, on a whim, I signed up for a place in the Great North Run. I reasoned that, if others could do it, maybe it was within my reach. I owned an old pair of trainers, no running shoes. On Mothers' Day 2005, with six months to move from being a non-runner to completing a half marathon, I took my first steps as a runner. I set out early, confident that I could be out and back before anyone noticed I was missing. Cold March air hit my face and hammered into my lungs as I gasped and wheezed my way to the top of the road. Just a few paces behind me and I was ready to give up, acknowledge it wasn't for me. I might have done so but for a cheery 'Good morning, are you off for a run?' from a neighbour returning from an even earlier dog walk. I staggered on, maintaining a running motion until I was safely around the corner and out of view. With more walking than running, I stayed out for twenty minutes, covering a much shorter distance than I'd planned. Day after day, for the next few weeks, I maintained the habit. I built up quickly to cover a 3 mile route, learning to set off slowly, keep going at a steady pace. At first, I encouraged myself to run just to the next lamppost and then the next before I gifted myself the luxury of a short walk. Eventually I was running the full route, working towards a pace where I could manage the circuit in just over half an hour. I was running consistent ten minute miles, respectable for a newcomer, until my lack of running shoes began to take its toll. Excruciating pain hit my shins and Achilles tendons. Once again, I was ready to give up.

Public commitment, and a charity place, kept me going. I could barely walk as I made my way to the running shop for advice and more supportive shoes. I maintained my training and by September, I'd completed my first half-marathon. Supporters shouted encouragement for all of the 13.1 miles. Crowds lined the Tyne Bridge. From Gateshead to South Shields, they offered refreshments: sweets, fruit and cakes; even home brewed beer. I declined. It was going well. Towards the end, I suffered a cramp, stopped, stretched, then sprinted too soon when I saw the sea. It's a tough mile-and-a-bit along the coast to the finish.

It wasn't easy, but I caught the bug. No longer a novice, I'd discovered the joy of running. From sneaking out in the early hours, hoping not to be seen, I'd become a runner. I learned to welcome the greetings of friends and other runners. Even hecklers, firmly wedged behind their steering wheels, couldn't spoil the pleasure of a solitary run.

Approaching my sixtieth birthday, with many half-marathons behind me, I rose to the challenge of couch based commentators speaking of 'only' half-marathons and signed up for the full 26.2 miles.

'I'll do it once,' I said, 'just once.'

Determined to train properly and enjoy every step of the way, I ran through the hottest of summers. Training wasn't easy; but the prospect of 26.2 miles motivated me to work at getting at least the first twenty into my comfort zone. To run long distances before the day became too hot, I set my alarm early and was out running well before my normal breakfast time. For longer runs, I'd take the first train into Leeds, set off beside the canal and enjoy the thrill as mileposts ticked off my steps towards Liverpool. I ran away from offices, through the city's industrial heritage into the countryside beyond. Cool water and shady trees lined the edges of my route as I ran towards the locks at Bingley. One morning, two sprinters thundered towards me, the towpath shuddered beneath their feet as they greeted me. I was training with the best, gold and silver medallists, the Brownlee brothers.

It wasn't all highs, there were lows of training too. As other grannies worried about 'having falls,' this granny became actively engaged in running falls. Our town is surrounded by grassland; two hundred acres, give or take the bits shaved off over the years for traffic flow. In early spring, the grass comes to life with crocuses, later in the season it's criss-crossed with cherry blossom. In recent years, the trees have become a tourist magnet. A canopy of pink blossom against blue skies creates a beautiful backdrop for selfies and more formal portraits. On a perfect day, not only for running but for sightseeing too, it was busy with dog walkers, couples, families, office workers with their sandwiches. It created the ideal setting for a granny, breaking in new running shoes, to trip over the tarmac and crash to earth, skidding along the ground on hands, knees and elbows. My very active fall was no doubt caught in many pictures. 'No, I'm fine,' I lied to the young man rushing towards me to assess the damage. With super-granny effort, I dragged myself up and forced myself into a slow jog to hobble the rest of the way home. The bruises were awesome; my hands are damaged. I don't run on my hands. So long as my knees don't fail me, I'll be a runner.

The long hot summer of training ended on marathon day. The weather broke with a vengeance, there was no risk of overheating that day, the first few miles were spent avoiding puddles. Later, roads turned into rivers, streams of runners splashed their way around York's villages. I broke no records, I'd been running for five hours before I turned to climb the hill back towards the university. With my fundraising hashtag, #thisgrannyruns, printed onto my rain-soaked vest, I was everybody's granny as the cheers of the crowd echoed from beneath umbrellas, carrying me towards a final descent to the finish. Exhausted and exhilarated, I relished the moment. I'd loved every sodden step. I'd run my marathon, laid the ghost of 'just' a half. I've no plans to run another.

Body and mind are intertwined. I'm inspired by Murakami; when I'm not running, my writing fades a little too. The rhythm and solitude of running defines my thinking space. The breathing in and breathing out required to maintain a steady pace unravels my thoughts. I take ideas and run with them. I find words as I run, they tumble, jumbled into my consciousness. As I stride out they form perfectly crafted sentences in my mind. Sometimes I remember them, carry them home, and place them on a page.

I'm a runner, one of more stamina than speed, I owe it to my mind, every bit as much as to my body. I've recently invested in a new pair of my favourite running shoes. They'll not get to carry me through another marathon, not even just a half, but they'll do their work in solitary striding and reward me in my writing.

Sally Arkinstall

Blackwater Alabama

you drive along a dirt road. gravel, deerskin, the smell of rot. paint peels from the walls in great long strips and you think that if you drive far enough you might escape some of it, but you're drunk and it is sunday. your ribcage opens and a thousand dead things crawl out. july seeps into something hot like death between your teeth, and you must be screaming with your shoulders back and your teeth bared because no one is answering. the sun bares down on you like rage. since we came from the dirt does that mean we must swallow it? you think of your mother and the piano that is never in tune and you spit dirt from your mouth on the highway. the taste is like something rotten but it must be right because why else would they have put you on your hands and knees and pushed your head to the floor if not to taste it? you think about whether you are still going to heaven and your eyes bleed from the corners. bruised knees, the scrape of wood that's splintered in the middle. you pray to god even though you know He cannot hear you, or maybe he can, but you're drunk and it is sunday and there is never any answer. you breathe in mildew and bleed on purpose. you crawl outside of your skin just to hear yourself.

Amelie Woodwards

my mind is like a tangerine

we find them at the farmer's market, a pound for a bushel,
   each the size of a palm. you tuck them in your pocket like
   a secret.
i find later, as you hold them, that the skin is dimpled,
   bruised. you pluck the stem and caress it in your palm,
   tenderly, encouragingly.
i expect the next part to hurt, breaking the surface, thumb
   digging in, rind beneath the nail, but you are soft-handed. i
   mould beneath your touch.
it's a careful peeling. i watch as you undo the layers, pith –
   like webbing: a shroud of protection, the skin pulled back
   from the body.
the whole unleashed. sliced into parts – into carpels, you tell
   me. spilling out.
that sour scent of exposure. clinging. creeping. closer to the
   centre.
you pick the pips: like cancer, festering, bitter reminders.
   uproot them, they do you no good. why cling onto
   something so bad?
why cling onto something so bad?
when something so toothsome lies at its centre – like nectar,
   or ambrosia, this sweet secretion. it drips from your lips
   like honey, pulp pressed against your tongue.
the mind is like a tangerine, you tell me:
to savour the sweetness within,
one must let the bitter thoughts flee.

Amy Platt

Strange Man by My Bed

I'm starting to get tired of always and repeatedly
Losing my marbles. The ones soaked in glass splendour and
 doused in divine memory.
My hands have been searching in the garden, in the cemetery.
 Tracing fingers over my
Mind but they are lost in formality, brutality, and that
 stuffing in between.

I'm starting to peel off my skin, so I can see better, and I'm
 being seen.
Losing a labyrinth game but when you smile at me, I think
My, what a beautiful boy and a glimmer of my marble peaks
 from your
Mind. I reach for it, behind your ear but it is gone and you're
 not really here.

I'm starting to think that this strange man by my bed wants
 to take something dear.
Losing my days is one thing but don't take my memories too.
My childhood of beads, chubby chalk fingers and glass
 scented skin.
Mind you, his eyes look familiar though. Like the boy I used
 to know.

I'm starting to miss how my boys played in the snow.
Losing their mittens, hats, and socks. They're out still
 searching.
My feet try and take me there, but I'm stuck in this place.
 Strange
Mind of mine imagines them under layers of faces that blur
 under fog.

I'm starting to call for my favourite dog.
Losing her toy under the couch makes her quiet.
My hands cannot find it, and my voice calls her name. Never
Mind she's probably as deaf and tired as me.

I'm starting to hum a little off key
Losing the lyrics to that lovely song
My husband would sing so beautifully. Frail
Mind, help me keep him young, so I don't forget

I'm starting to regret
Losing my boys to these men
My how they've grown
Mind your manners strange man.

I'm starting to anger at the way he sang
Losing his voice like
My husband did.
Mind you his eyes...

I'm starting to cry
Losing
My boys in the snow...
Mind please work.

I'm going berserk
Losing
My lovely
Mind

I'm
Losing
My
Mind

Aimee Wade

The Lift

The door is invitingly open. I feel compelled to enter and step into a hallway flooded with light. Black and white floor tiling leads past a porter's desk towards a deeply carpeted staircase that, after only a few steps, curves sharply around and disappears from view. A porter emerges from behind a door. Dressed in a bottle green jacket with gold braiding on the breast pocket, he stands tall, like a soldier on duty. He looks me up and down.

'Good morning Miss. The stairs are just in front of you but I'd strongly recommend you take the lift.' He looks down immediately and begins to write in the large, red, leather-bound book on his desk.

Sight of the lift makes the stairs an extremely attractive option. It is an ancient Victorian contraption that looks like an intricate cage, only the back section being solid enough to hold a gold mirror adorned with cherubs peeking out from intricate frippery. The remaining sides are constructed of ornate lattice iron work, barely robust enough to protect any occupants from falling out. I cough nervously and look back at the porter.

'The lift, if you please Miss.'

I want to say that I really do need to take the stairs but there appears to be no room for negotiation. Entering the lift feels like a major step into the unknown, only a flimsy floor between me and sudden death or, at best, life changing injuries. I pull the rickety-rackety door, which unfolds itself to meet a latch on the opposite side. There is a reassuring click as the door locks.

'Press any floor you like.' The porter's voice booms down the hallway.

The buttons indicate a choice of three floors: 'Entry', the ground floor I am on, a floor above and one below labelled 'Basemeant.' It seems strange to me that such a carefully managed place should allow a spelling mistake. The floor labelled 'Transcendence' is the most intriguing and I hold my finger on the button waiting to be propelled to the top.

What happens next is totally unexpected. Instead of taking a juddery journey upwards, I hurtle downwards at speed into the deepest darkness. No time to think or act, I can only hold on to what support I have and allow myself to be taken somewhere I have not chosen to go. My heart pounds with fright, my mind in complete meltdown and my stomach lurches as the lift plunges further and further into the depths. I slide down the back wall and collapse onto the floor. As I brace myself for the inevitable the lift starts to slow down, rattling and shaking until it thuds to an abrupt halt. Not trusting myself to get up, I watch as the door to the lift unlocks itself and opens.

'Welcome to Basemeant, I am sorry if it is not where you expected to be.' A disembodied voice echoes through the darkness.

As I raise myself from the floor, shaking and confused, I catch a glimpse of my face in the mirror. It is unrecognisable. I am desperate to get out of the place but despite furiously banging all the buttons with my closed fist, the lift does not move.

'I'm afraid it's no good trying to leave.' The voice is not unkind but it is firm. 'You must stay a while.'

Suddenly the word 'Basemeant' appears, writ large in bright yellow neon. The light illuminates a simple, wooden chair.

'Please, take a seat.'

Thankfully, the chair is close to the lift and I move towards it and sit, grateful for some solidity beneath my feet.

'It has come to our attention that, despite strong messages to the contrary, you have been carrying on for a considerable time as if everything is alright; 'fine' is a word you use a great deal. Is that right?'

Any resistance within me has been knocked out by the journey but, making my voice as strong as possible, I muster a response,

'I don't know what you mean, who are you, where am I?'

'My apologies again, I should have introduced myself. I am 'Mind,' and this place is known as 'Basemeant.' It's a poor play on words I know but essentially it is the lowest place anyone can get to and the one people are most afraid of. 'Basemeant' is however a critical stopping off point, somewhere you must spend time in before you can make any changes for the better.'

'But why am I here.' The whole thing made no sense at all.

'Because you have reached rock-bottom. Heart and Body have been trying to stop you but are now too depleted and cannot support you any further.' The voice sounded annoyed. 'It's always the same, no matter how loudly I try to be heard, people switch me off, sometimes they drug me in order not to hear.'

I pretend I don't understand what Mind is referring to but, deep inside, I know that so often I have heard my internal voice telling me to 'stop,' 'take time out', 'you can't be everything to everybody'. Instead, I insert new mantras about how strong I am and how I must strive for perfection in everything at all costs. I am worn out but have refused to listen and accept the fact.

Mind encourages me to speak out how exhausted I am, and I do so, hearing my words disappear into the darkness and, as feared, all the feelings that I have been trying to hold at bay sweep over me and I panic, overwhelmed and unsteady. It's the very place I do not want to be and I hide my face in my hands, ashamed by my weakness. Mind's voice cuts through the pain.

'Don't worry, what you are experiencing is usual. Heart is heavy with emotion and has been waiting a long time to let go. That's why it feels too much. It is what people are most afraid of, that's why they do everything to avoid coming here. The pain won't last forever and, in having the courage to acknowledge it exists, you will make room for something more real and sustaining to move in. And it will.'

I can hear the words but I worry the weeping will never stop. I have no idea how long I cry for but eventually the wracking sobs subside and, when they cease, Mind speaks again.

'Well done, you walked across the threshold and found Basemeant before you were forced to. Often people leave it too late. Everyone must come here at least once in their lives, occasionally more often, it is a necessary part of living not a place to be afraid of, but always people want to head straight to 'Transcendence,' as you did. I'm afraid, you can't get there without coming here first. You must learn to love the shadow along with the light, both are essential to live a whole life.'

That I did the right thing by crossing the threshold of the open door is deeply comforting but I do not want to stay where I am for much longer.

'What is there in "Transcendence," and can I go there now?'

'Transcendence is a place of light and air, where the Heart

and Body are in charge. Next time, the lift will take you straight to the third floor. But not yet, there must be a period of rehearsing your new way of being so that, as Mind, I am convinced there will be an alignment when you meet Heart and Body. We are so often set in conflict with one another and none of us like it. Do you understand?'

'I think so and I will try.' I didn't sound convincing to myself.

'There is no good just trying.' Mind spoke definitively. 'Otherwise, you will end up back here again and not ever get to 'Transcendence' and that's not what either of us want at all.'

As I assured Mind that I did understand, I would be different and this time I meant it. I felt a renewed energy, a spotlight burst through the gloom and danced around me, the air became warmer and it felt as if I was being embraced. The lift doors rattled.

'Time to go now and don't worry, Mind is always on your side.'

The journey back to 'Entry' seemed to take only seconds. I blinked as I stepped into the luminosity of the hall.

'Hello Miss, welcome back, looking forward to seeing you again soon. Straight to the top next time.' The porter winked and smiled encouragingly.

'I'll look forward to it.'

I smiled back at him as I headed towards the open door. It felt as if I had been away for ages but everything outside looked the same as when I arrived. What was different was me and I knew it would not be too long before the top floor was well within my reach.

Claire Maxwell

Credits – Beyond the Walls Team 2025

Editorial and Production

Ethan Black, Josh Clough, Sophie Foster, Becca Green,
Jessica Lawrence, Reece Linley, Phoebe Porritt, James Sales,
Rhydian Snowden and Holly Walker.

Blogs and Podcasts

Morgan Adams, Eryca Ducker, Elisha Greenwood,
Estelle Hardman, Oliver Lewis, Faye Simpson
and Rose Williams.

Marketing and Events

Elizabeth Airriess, Paige Brownbill, Hayley Coleman,
Emily Horne, Eleanor Matthews, Elizabeth St James,
Phoebe Vines and Aimee Wade.

Cover Artwork

Aimee Wade.